D1019095

TWAYNE'S WORLD AUTHORS SERIES

A Survey of the World's Literature

Sylvia E. Bowman, Indiana University

GENERAL EDITOR

SPAIN

Janet W. Díaz, University of North Carolina, Chapel Hill
Gerald Wade, Vanderbilt University

EDITORS

Juan Pablo Forner

TWAS 377

JUAN PABLO FORNER

By GILBERT SMITH
North Carolina State University

TWAYNE PUBLISHERS

A DIVISION OF G. K. HALL & CO., BOSTON

Library of Congress Cataloging in Publication Data
Smith, Gilbert, 1937-
  Juan Pablo Forner.

  (Twayne's world authors series ; TWAS 377 : Spain)
  Bibliography: p. 147-58.
  Includes index.
  1.   Forner, Juan Pablo, 1756-1797 — Criticism and
interpretation.
PQ6523.F5Z88   868'.4'09   75-33832
ISBN 0-8057-6170-5

For Juan López-Morillas and John Howie
maestros par excellence

Contents

About the Author

Gilbert Smith was born in Anson, Texas, in 1937, and holds degrees from Baylor, Tulane, and Brown Universities. He has taught at Wake Forest, Vanderbilt, and North Carolina State University. He has received a number of grants to support his scholarly investigations, and has published articles on the literature of the medieval and modern periods in Spain. His writing has appeared in *Anales Galdosianos, Hispania, Judaism, Modern Language Journal, Modern Language Notes, Revista de Estudios Hispánicos*, and *South Atlantic Quarterly*. He was a consultant on Spanish authors for the 1974 edition of the *Encyclopaedia Britannica* and serves as managing editor of the *North Carolina Foreign Language Review*. He is presently completing a book on the novelist Benito Pérez Galdós, based on unpublished materials in the Casa-Museo Pérez Galdós in Las Palmas de Gran Canaria. His interest in Juan Pablo Forner has led him into research on the presence of Cervantes in eighteenth-century literature and criticism, which will be the subject of his next book.

Preface

Juan Pablo Forner has always been a controversial figure in the history of Spanish literature. His career spanned only about fifteen years (1782 - 97) and he produced only one work still considered important to a study of the literature of eighteenth-century Spain, the *Exequias de la lengua castellana* (*Funeral Rite for the Castilian Language*). One of the many paradoxes of Forner's career is that, in spite of his having contributed so little to the "official canon" of Spanish literature, a study of his professional activities inevitably encompasses the work of every significant writer in Spain from 1782 to 1797. He was the most prolific of those writers in one area — the literary polemic — and, in the opinion of many, he was by far the writer with the sharpest wit, the keenest sense of humor, and the greatest ingenuity.

Forner has been controversial because he consistently employed those talents in an acrid satire that many critics and literary historians find offensive, while others excuse it because of Forner's ultraconservative ideology. In this book I have tried to remain objective about the personal nature of Forner's literary activities. I believe that his life and work are fascinating precisely because he was so controversial, and because his work provides a kind of compendium of the late eighteenth century in Spain.

I have omitted from this study a large part of Forner's writings, for several reasons. I have not dealt with the treatises on law and history, because they have very little relationship to his production in belles-lettres. I have chosen to deal with Forner's poetry only to the extent that it provides some insight into his other works. With the exception of a few poems, his extensive poetic work was not published during his lifetime and did not have the repercussions in manuscript form that many of his unpublished prose works did. The poetry is undistinguished and adds little to an understanding of Forner's significance as a writer.

I am grateful to the Vanderbilt University Research Council for a grant that gave me the opportunity to begin my study of Forner several years ago. In the course of my research, I have become indebted to the enlightened Hispanist George Ticknor for having the foresight over a century ago to collect the rare pamphlets and books related to eighteenth-century polemics; to the Boston Public Library for its wisdom in preserving the Ticknor collection; to María Jiménez Salas, whose book on Forner provides invaluable documentation; and to Emilio Cotarelo y Mori, whose study of Iriarte is among the finest products of Hispanic scholarship.

I hope that this study of Forner and the late eighteenth-century literary milieu will meet the ideal of that century: that it will be both instructive and entertaining.

GILBERT SMITH

Raleigh, North Carolina

Chronology

1756   February 17: Forner is born in Mérida.

1765   Forner goes to Madrid to live with his uncle, Andrés Piquer, and receives his early education from Francisco Torrecilla.

1771 -   Forner attends the Universities of Salamanca and Toledo,
1775   and becomes a friend of Juan Meléndez Valdés and José Iglesias de la Casa.

1778   Forner begins law studies at the Institute of San Isidro in Madrid.

1780   Meléndez Valdés wins over Tomás de Iriarte in the Royal Academy's competition for an eclogue. Iriarte criticizes the decision in the *Reflexiones sobre la égloga intitulada "Batilo"* (*Reflections Concerning the Eclogue Entitled "Batilo"*).

1781   Forner attacks Iriarte's *Reflections* and praises Meléndez' poem in a *Cotejo de las églogas* (*Comparison of the Eclogues*).

1782   Forner satirizes Iriarte in *El asno erudito* (*The Erudite Ass*) and *Los gramáticos: historia chinesca* (*The Grammarians: A Chinese History*). In October, Forner wins the academy prize for his *Sátira contra los vicios introducidos en la poesía castellana* (*Satire Against the Vices Introduced Into Castilian Poetry*).

1783   Forner enters the law school of the Institute of San Isidro. Masson de Morvilliers portrays Spain as "the most ignorant nation in Europe" in the *Encyclopédie Méthodique* (*Encyclopedia of Method*), published in Paris. Forner's *Grammarians* is censured and seized by the authorities.

1784   Forner criticizes Trigueros in the *Carta de Don Antonio Varas* (*Letter From Don Antonio Varas*), which is denounced by the Council of Castilla. López de Ayala, the censor, rejects Forner's play, *La cautiva española* (*The Spanish Captive Girl*). Forner responds with his *Carta . . . a Don Ignacio López de Ayala* (*Letter . . . to Don Ignacio López de Ayala*), in which he attacks Huerta's play, *Raquel*.

1785   The Royal Academy rejects Forner's *Oración apologética por la España y su mérito literario* (*Apologetic Oration for Spain and Her Literary Merit*). Two major works appear: Sempere's *Ensayo de una biblioteca española de los mejores escritores del reynado de Carlos III* (*Essay on a Spanish Library of the Best Writers of the Reign of Charles III*) and Huerta's *Theatro Hespañol* (*Spanish Theater*).

1786   Carlo Denina delivers his rebuttal to Masson before the Berlin Academy. Forner publishes Denina's address with his own *Apologetic Oration* as a preface. Huerta replies to criticism of the *Spanish Theater* with the *Lección crítica* (*Lesson in Criticism*), in which he calls Forner *tuerto* (one-eyed). Forner answers with the *Reflexiones . . . [de] Tomé Cecial* (*Reflections . . . [of] Tomé Cecial*).

1787   Forner publishes the *Discursos filosóficos sobre el hombre* (*Philosophical Discourses Concerning Man*), a long poem with copious notes written in 1780 [?]. Forner defends his *Apologetic Oration* in the *Antisofisma* (*Antisophistry*).

1788   Forner writes the *Exequias de la lengua castellana* (*Funeral Rite for the Castilian Language*), for which he never finds a publisher.

1789   Sempere attacks Forner in an article on Trigueros in volume six of the *Library of the Best Writers*. Forner answers with a *Suplemento al artículo "Trigueros"* (*Supplement to the Article "Trigueros"*). Forner becomes involved in a polemic with Tomás Antonio Sánchez, and publishes the *Carta de Bartolo* (*Letter From Bartolo*).

1790   Forner defends Leandro Fernández de Moratín's play, *El viejo y la niña* (*The Old Man and the Maiden*), in a letter to the *Correo de Madrid* (*Madrid Dispatch*), signed Lorenzo Garrote.

1791   Forner is named public defender in Seville and marries María del Carmen Carassa. He is elected to various honorary societies and academies. The polemics cease for three years.

1795   Forner's *Funeral Rite* is rejected by the censor as inappropriate because of the critical political situation. Forner's *La corneja sin plumas* (*The Featherless Crow*) accuses José Vargas y Ponce of plagiarism. Forner becomes involved in a polemic over the theater with the clerics of Seville, and publishes the *Preservativo contra el ateísmo* (*Preservative Against Atheism*) in defense of his own orthodoxy.

1796   Forner's play, *La escuela de la amistad, o el filósofo enamorado* (*School for Friendship, or The Enamored Philosopher*), opens in Madrid with some success. Forner moves to Madrid, where he has been named public defender of the Council of Castilla. He publishes *La paz* (*The Peace*), a poem in praise of Godoy, the Prince of the Peace.

1797   March 16: Forner dies in Madrid. On May 23, Joaquín María Sotelo reads an adulatory eulogy of Forner before the Royal Academy of Law.

1798   Sotelo's eulogy is published in Madrid.

CHAPTER 1

The Early Years

JUAN PABLO FORNER was born in Mérida, Spain, on February 17, 1756.[1] His father, Francisco Forner y Segarra, was a physician and his mother, Manuela Piquer y Zaragosa, was the niece of Andrés Piquer, a well-known scholar and professor of medicine who was at one time the personal physician of King Fernando VI. When Forner's mother died in 1765, he was sent to Madrid to live with Piquer, who directed his early education and placed him under the tutelage of Francisco Torrecilla, an illustrious professor of grammar and Latin. Forner's later education included study at the Universities of Salamanca and Toledo from 1771 to 1775, and the study of law at the Institute of San Isidro in Madrid from 1778 to 1783, when he entered the law school of the institute. During these years back in Madrid, Forner lived in the home of Juan Crisóstomo Piquer, the son of Andrés.

I The Influence of Andrés Piquer

Forner first gained public attention in 1782 by satirizing the literature of his contemporaries, and spent his entire career engaged in disputes with other writers. His relationship to the Piquer family had a significant influence on the development of the attitudes that he expressed in his polemical works. In the *Obras póstumas* (*Posthumous Works*) of Andrés Piquer, published in 1785 by Juan Crisóstomo, there is a discourse delivered by Piquer in 1770 entitled "Informe de la Academia Médica-matritense al supremo Consejo de Castilla sobre censores de libros" ("Report of the Madrid Medical Academy to the Supreme Council of Castilla Concerning Censors of Books"). In this address, Piquer sets forth the principal maxim that "if a book is to be useful and advantageous to the public, it must promote the glory of God and the good of human society."[2] Every book approved for publication must affirm traditional Catholic

15

dogma and contribute to the good of society by telling a truth "useful to the readers, to religion, and to the state."[3] Piquer explains that this censorship of books is necessary, because the common people "cannot discern truth from error, and, seeing something in print, believe a superstition as readily as an article of faith."[4] Thus, strict regulation of printed material is necessary to enable man to achieve the two things that he always strives for, "things essential to the conservation of his being and his well-being; that is, eternal happiness, which he gains through religion, and temporal happiness, which he achieves through his relationship with society."[5]

These ideas are not unusual, for they coincide with the "official position" on censorship in eighteenth-century Spain. It is significant, however, that they are expressed so clearly in the writings of Piquer, who was responsible for Forner's early education. Forner surely was aware of this address on censorship, for he was living with Piquer at the time that it was delivered. Also, Juan Crisóstomo was probably preparing this edition of his father's work while Forner was living in his home in the early 1780s. The ideas expressed by Piquer also appear frequently in Forner's writings: because the common people are vulnerable to error, their reading material must be regulated in order to insure their happiness, which depends on a right relationship to God and to society. In 1783 Forner himself acknowledged his debt to his mother's uncle: "I have had no diversion or entertainment in my life other than books and meditation. Separated from the company of people, denying public life, I have applied myself insofar as possible to cultivating my understanding. I owe my instruction in philosophy to the late Andrés Piquer, my maternal uncle, in whose house and in the shadow of whom I was reared."[6]

II   *The Salamanca* Tertulia

Throughout his life, Forner maintained the conservative attitudes that guided his early education. These attitudes surely determined to some extent the kind of people that he chose to associate with, and those associates in turn had an influence on the direction that his career took. During the Salamanca years (1771 - 74), Forner participated in a *tertulia* — a regular meeting of friends to socialize and discuss common interests — organized by Fray Diego González, an active literary figure. This group included Juan Meléndez Valdés and José Iglesias de la Casa. Meléndez Valdés was yet an unknown writer at the time of the Salamanca *tertulia*, but he later became one of the important poets of eighteenth-century Spain and was instrumental in Forner's first public recognition. Iglesias was one of the few men with whom Forner maintained a lasting friendship.

Forner did not have many friends, probably because of his acrid personality. His choice of Iglesias as a companion is explained by this description of the poet offered by Miguel de la Pinta Llorente in a study of cultural trends in Forner's time: "Don José Iglesias de la Casa [was] . . . a priest, musician, painter, and sculptor, [and] the author of very popular epigrams and poems written before he took his vows. . . . His writings are characterized by a great purity of language and his chaste genius immunized him against foreign modes. . . . His case is most certainly singular, a poet . . . free of the Frenchified currents navigated by almost all the intellectuals and poets of his time."[7] This could well be a characterization of Forner's ambition: to be pure in language, chaste of genius, and free of Frenchified currents.

The influence of Iglesias is evident in Forner's most important work, the *Exequias de la lengua castellana* (*Funeral Rite for the Castilian Language*). In the Salamanca group, Forner and Iglesias used the poetic names Aminta and Arcadio, and in the *Funeral Rite* — written about 1788 — Aminta and Arcadio make a pilgrimage to Parnassus to attend the last rites of the Castilian language, put to death by careless writers who strayed from pure linguistic expression. Their guide to the mountain of the gods is none other than Miguel de Cervantes, who two centuries earlier had written his own *Viaje del Parnaso* (*Voyage to Parnassus*).[8] When Arcadio asks if he is worthy of participating in the pilgrimage, Cervantes' reply reveals the reasons that Forner found Iglesias to be such an agreeable companion. These lines also summarize the fundamental points of the polemical activity in which Forner engaged throughout his career.

Of course you may [accompany us] . . . , provided that you are of the good sect, that is:

> If a booklet from France
> translated you've not,
> nor our language enhanced
> with gallicized glott;
> Nor prose-poems devised
> in tragedies feigned,
> whose brave Cismontane[9]

just bores us to death
before his last breath
sets off his demise;
    Nor extended your reach
to enfable our speech
by copying coldness
because of the boldness
of Parisian abundance
of fable-redundance;
    Nor polished your diction
with esprit so in vogue,
thus making resplendent
Castilian a fiction
that rows with a brogue;
    Nor been too dependent
on mosiac composition
to boast versatility
and inlaid ability
in hodge-podge competition;
    Then welcome indeed,
to Parnassus proceed,
where change cannot thrive;
let decorum proclaim
its resolute aim:
good taste will survive.

(*Ningún inconveniente hay en ello . . . con tal que seáis de la buena secta,
esto es:*

Si nunca habéis traducido
Algún librito de Francia,
Copiando gálicas frases
Con españolas palabras;
    Si no habéis hecho tragedias
De prosa que mal se inflama;
En que el héroe Cismontano
Antes que muera, nos mata;
    Si porque en París se encuentran
Fábulas en abundancia,
No enfabuláis el idioma
Con frialdades imitadas;
    Si de un esprit que está en boga
Nunca espiritáis el habla,
Haciendo que bogue y reme
La magestad castellana;
    Si no escribís taraceas

Cual de estructura mosaica,
Y por mostraros pantojo,
No publicáis mezcolanzas;
   Enhorabuena al Parnaso
Venid, donde las mudanzas
No llegan, y eternamente
Su ser el buen gusto guarda.)[10]

This denunciation of eighteenth-century Spain's tendency to imitate French language and literature is representative of the anti-Gallic orientation of almost everything that Forner wrote. Through the words of Arcadio and Aminta, the *Funeral Rite* presents a compendium of Forner's attitudes concerning the inane literature of the last decades of the eighteenth century, the "coldness" of the literature, the hodge-podge writing, and the paucity of good taste. Throughout his career, Forner attributed these faults to French influence, and very early he established himself as the most important spokesman for the anti-French point of view.

III   *The Madrid* Tertulia

This Gallophobic attitude obviously had some official sanction, for the Royal Spanish Academy gave Forner the first prize in its 1782 poetry competition for his *Sátira contra los vicios introducidos en la poesía castellana* (*Satire Against the Vices Introduced Into Castilian Poetry*), in which he criticized the same things that he later satirized in the *Funeral Rite*. Three months before he received this award, Forner had attracted a great deal of attention by publishing *El asno erudito* (*The Erudite Ass*), a fable satirizing Tomás de Iriarte, one of the most important literary figures in Spain at the time.

It was *The Erudite Ass* that launched Forner's career and started the long polemic with Iriarte that I will discuss in the next chapter. The *Satire Against the Vices Introduced Into Castilian Poetry* had fewer repercussions, but it did have one very important effect: it put him in contact with some influential people in Madrid. The second prize in that academy competition went to Don Leandro Fernández de Moratín, who later became one of Spain's foremost poets and playwrights. Moratín wanted to meet Forner, and Pedro Estala, an important literary figure, arranged a meeting for them. That meeting turned into a regular *tertulia* frequented by Forner, Moratín, the Abbott Melón, Eustache Fernández de Navarrete, León de Arroyal, and Luis de Godoy — the brother of Manuel, future secretary of state to Charles IV and Prince of the Peace.[11]

Like the earlier Salamanca group, this gathering enabled Forner to associate with important literary and public figures. Estala later participated in Forner's attempts to produce his plays, and Manuel Godoy's influence was very important in the last years of Forner's life. Forner's activities within this group of well-established intellectuals indicate that he was an aggressive and convincing individual. They were planning to publish a dictionary of the illustrious men of the day, but Forner insisted that they work instead toward the publication of the biblical dissertations of Padre Calmet. The fact that they started on the project, even though they never finished it, suggests that Forner had a strong influence in spite of his youth and his relative unimportance at that time.

While these men were serious writers concerned with the refinement of literature, they did have their less solemn moments. Antonio Papell reports that José Antonio Conde joined the group after he lost his seat as professor of Hebrew and Greek at the University of Alcalá for having composed a hymn of questionable orthodoxy. The group arrogantly responded to the Inquisition's censure of Conde by singing the hymn at their meetings. They also wrote a half-serious, half-satirical constitution for their "academy." This constitution is obviously something of a joke, but some of the ideas included in it are fundamental to the ideology of Forner.

> The academy will not give a damn about knowing if its members are Old Christians or bald ones, rancid or fresh, raw or poached. . . . The proofs and reports required for the admission of an individual will rest on his doctrine, and on nothing else. . . . The only affirmation demanded of each individual will be that he detests the semi-Gallic sect, and will defend with blood and fire the true Castilian good taste, in prose and in verse. And therefore, he will be required to promote allegiance to our good writers of the sixteenth and seventeenth centuries, and they will be his only goal and guide. If, to the disgrace of the academy, some men of a scatterbrained and perverse taste should try to gain admission . . . they will be made to understand that they must enter only in order to learn and be judged until they lose the aroma of their first style.[12]

These men, then, were all of one mind, and Forner — one of the signers of this constitution — was surely a powerful force among them. An incident that occurred in the Madrid group indicates that he elicited a fierce loyalty from his friends. Forner became involved in a dispute with León de Arroyal, a dispute for which the reasons were never clear. The *tertulia* sided with Forner, who was to build an entire career on vicious, personal attacks on everyone with whom he disagreed. The dispute with Arroyal must have been extremely bitter, for in Forner's notebooks there is a poem — an epitaph for Arroyal's father — which is in poor taste, to say the least.

> In this, not frigid urn,
> but eternal shade's black gape
> Fernando de Arroyal dissolvèd lies.
> Because he lived he perished,
> his body, to dust now turned,
> (gone the external shape
> as man he cherished)
> in another form survives.
> To our world his name
> matters not; to him neither fame
> of epitaph nor Mausoleum great
> was of import, but his fate
> of escape from death triumphantly won.
> His versifying son
> (to make him — he claimed —
> immortal) atop what remained
> cast an epigram so fierce
> that he managed to pierce,
> to destroy and to goad,
> weighing his brow
> with weightier load
> than the gravestone's plow.
> This thing we pray:
> (if the corpse, now nought,
> from human pity pleasure reaps
> in this brief space wherein he sleeps)
> upon him lay
> and lightly weigh
> what his son has wrought.

> (*Fernando de Arroyal yace disuelto*
> *en esta, no urna fría,*
> *mas hoya oscura de tiniebla eterna:*
> *Murió porque vivía,*
> *y el cuerpo en polvo vuelto*
> *tomó otra forma si perdió la externa*
> *que mantuvo cual hombre;*
> *poco al mundo su nombre*
> *le importa; y a él tan solo*
> *no epitafio, no vano Mauseolo,*

sino la augusta suerte
de escapar con victoria de la muerte.
Tuvo un hijo Coplero
que un epigrama fiero
echó sobre el cadáver miserable
tal, que pensando hacerle perdurable,
con la carga asombrosa
pudo más destruirle que la losa.
Si al cuerpo que ya es nada
la humana compasión tal vez le agrada,
aquí reposa en este espacio breve,
su hijo Don León le sea leve.)[13]

This satirical poem is an excellent example of the kind of activity that Forner engaged in throughout his career. His fame was almost entirely the result of his caustic commentaries on the works of other writers, and those commentaries were manifestations of the attitudes acquired through his early training and reinforced by his association with people like José Iglesias de la Casa.

CHAPTER 2

The Polemic With Iriarte

I *Meléndez Valdés and Iriarte*

O N two occasions, the annual poetry competition sponsored by the Royal Spanish Academy was instrumental in Forner's achieving public recognition. Forner's success in the 1782 contest led to his participation in the Madrid *tertulia*, and the 1780 competition also had important repercussions in his career. In that year Juan Meléndez Valdés, the friend from the Salamanca group, won the first prize for his *Batilo: égloga en alabanza de la vida del campo* (*Batilo: Eclogue in Praise of Country Life*). The second prize was given to Tomás de Iriarte for *La felicidad de la vida del campo* (*The Happiness of Country Life*), which was submitted under the pseudonym of Don Francisco Agustín de Cisneros.

The outcome of the 1780 competition surprised almost everyone, since Iriarte was the most famous literary figure in Spain and Meléndez was an unknown poet. In response to this embarrassing situation, Iriarte wrote and circulated in manuscript his *Reflexiones sobre la égloga intitulada "Batilo"* (*Reflections Concerning the Eclogue Entitled "Batilo"*), in which he criticized Meléndez' poem, praised his own, and condemned the academy for its decision. Even though Iriarte's poem had been published by the academy under his pseudonym, it was general knowledge that Cisneros was really Iriarte. Thus, his enemies immediately saw Iriarte's *Reflections* for what is was — the work of an author smarting from defeat and praising his own poem as he spoke out against the "injustice" of the academy's judgment.

II *Forner's Defense of Meléndez*

Forner's literary career began with a *Cotejo de las églogas que ha premiado la Academia Real de la Lengua* (*Comparison of the*

23

Eclogues Awarded Prizes by the Royal Academy of Language)
which he wrote and circulated among his friends. Forner compared
the two poems, as Iriarte had done in the *Reflections*, but came to
the opposite conclusion — that Meléndez' poem was better than the
eclogue by Cisneros, and that the academy should be commended
for its wise and just decision.

Forner had several reasons for responding to Iriarte's attack on
Meléndez. His friendship with Meléndez surely had something to
do with it, but his reaction was probably due more to his resentment
of Iriarte's unchallenged domination of the literary scene. Forner
wanted to establish himself as a writer, and nothing would bring
him to the attention of the public as rapidly as denouncing a well-
known literary figure like Iriarte. The *Comparison* is, for the most
part, a model of literary criticism. Forner sets forth the criteria by
which he will judge the two poems, and he then applies those
criteria to each poem systematically and objectively. However, this
literary criticism is accompanied by a number of sarcastic comments
about Iriarte himself. He speaks of the poet's "unawareness" of certain basic poetic principles and his "ignorance of the art in which he
tried to exercise his ability."[1] Forner ends the *Comparison* on a particularly nasty note:

Finally, the versification is not very correct and not at all simple. There is a
multitude of harsh and very disagreeable hiatuses. There is . . . but there is
nothing, for I believe that the author will attribute everything said here to
calumny and malediction. All in all, I beg the readers to apply the so-called
eclogue to the precepts that I have indicated, and they will see for
themselves. For I am exhausted from all this writing, and particularly about a
subject of so little importance.[2]

Although the *Comparison* was not published, the manuscript
found its way around the literary circles and was a delight to Iriarte's
many enemies. Iriarte had said in the *Reflections* that the academy
did not even know what a poem on country life was, and Forner
responded by saying that Iriarte did not even know what an eclogue
was. Forner even hinted that Iriarte was not a poet at all, that he
confused the most elementary principles of poetry, and that he was
not aware of the precepts so important to eighteenth-century poetic
art. According to Forner's judgment, Iriarte had tried to do
something that he simply was not prepared to do — write an
eclogue.

III   The Erudite Ass

In 1782 Iriarte published the work for which he would be best known, the *Fábulas literarias (Literary Fables)*. Iriarte claimed that his fables were entirely original, in that they dealt with literary subjects, something that the fable form had never done before. Many of the fables were interpreted as direct insults against certain literary figures of the day, including Forner. Forner immediately responded with a fable of his own, *The Erudite Ass*, which he published as an anonymous work with a prologue by the "publisher," Don Pablo Segarra.

The publication of *The Erudite Ass* was announced in the *Gazeta de Madrid (Madrid Gazette)* on July 12, 1782, and the fable rapidly became well known throughout Spain. It tells the story of Don Jumento (Don Ass), who knows that he is learned, but whose verses are not appreciated by a world that aspires to "gothicism."[3] Since he is surrounded by ignorant beasts incapable of understanding his erudition, he dresses up in a theatrical costume, complete with a wig to hide his ears and a cassock trimmed in gold, and appears before the beasts to introduce them to "science." As he talks, a fly becomes so bored with what he hears that he begins to buzz. The ass — who cannot overcome his innate tendencies — pricks up his ears, inadvertently lifting the wig off his head. As the animals begin to laugh, the fly stings the ass on the rear, and he brays so loudly that he can be heard in the Canary Islands. His costume falls off and he runs away, leaving the animals convulsed with laughter. The fable ends with a moral — the admonition that if anyone is stung by the story, it only proves that he is an ass; and that if someone sets out to write books, he should watch out for the flies.

In the long prologue to the fable, Segarra [Forner] insists that *The Erudite Ass* is not directed against anyone in particular, only against those poets who write commonplaces as if they were the greatest truths in the world. Yet the fable and its prologue contain so many obvious references to Iriarte that there can be no doubt that *The Erudite Ass* is a direct attack on the author of the *Literary Fables*. The ass in the fable quotes the first line of Iriarte's poem *Music* and boasts (as Iriarte did) of having written fables in Castilian in forty different meters; and the mention of the Canary Islands surely refers to Iriarte's birthplace, Tenerife. When Iriarte answered *The Erudite Ass* with *Para casos tales suelen tener los maestros oficiales (For Just Such Cases Do They Have Trained Teachers)*, he devoted the first ten pages to proving that Segarra was indeed directing the satire against him. *For Just Such Cases* was in the form of a letter from Don Eleuterio Geta, a friend writing to Iriarte defending him from Segarra's attack. In the prologue to *The Erudite Ass*, Segarra had referred to a letter from the Italian poet Metastasio which praised the poetry of the anonymous author of the fable. In response to this, Geta reprints a series of letters from Metastasio and from Iriarte's brothers Domingo and Bernardo, all praising the poem *Music* and reporting the favorable notices of Iriarte's poem in journals throughout Europe. Geta then comments that "this poet [Segarra] does not need Metastasio to praise him from Vienna; he himself takes on the very pleasant task of writing his own panegyric."[4]

Iriarte was right, of course. Forner had written his own panegyric in the prologue to the fable. What Iriarte did not say was that this was precisely what he himself had done in both *For Just Such Cases* and the *Reflections Concerning the Eclogue Entitled "Batilo."* In fact, Forner had actually imitated Iriarte's technique of using a pseudonym to praise himself in the *Reflections* when he created *The Erudite Ass*. This characteristic was common, both to this polemic as it continued, and to the other polemics in which Forner later became involved: one author made an attack; and the other responded with a work that imitated some trait of the first. In this way, each one attempted to make the other look ridiculous by turning the satirical devices around to work against the one who had initiated the attack. Forner's response to *For Just Such Cases* is a good example of this technique. Probably as a reply to Forner's criticism of Iriarte's use of language — one of the criticisms made in the *Comparison of the Eclogues* — Iriarte commented on Forner's use of archaic forms and peculiar grammatical constructions in *The Erudite Ass*. Forner replied with the bitterest and most extensive attack of his entire career, a vicious satire on the entire Iriarte family, *Los gramáticos: historia chinesca* (*The Grammarians: A Chinese History*).

IV *The Education of Iriarte*: The Grammarians

The Grammarians indicates how sensitive Forner was to any criticism of his use of language, for it is derived entirely from the fact that Iriarte had the audacity to give Forner a lesson in grammar. It tells the story of a young Chinese student who receives instruction from his elders on how to be a poet. He is taught that he must never sin against the rules of grammar, that exactitude is the greatest virtue of a poet, and that poetry must never surprise the reader with new truths. After some ridiculous ironic statements about what poetry should be, Forner ingeniously uses as an example Iriarte's own translation of Horace's *Ars poetica*. He also includes critiques of the "imperfect" poem, *Music*, and of the *Literary Fables*, as well as a defense of *The Erudite Ass*.

Iriarte's *For Just Such Cases* appeared in August 1782. *The Grammarians* must have been written very soon after that, because the manuscript was seized by the regent of Valencia on October 19. The censor in Valencia prohibited its publication, and it was not printed during Forner's lifetime. The most obvious reason for the suppression of *The Grammarians* is its libelous content. Forner gives names and specific references to the Iriartes to such an extent that this work is quite unlike his earlier, elusive attacks. But the actual censure of *The Grammarians* was the result of a strange coincidence. The Iriartes — Tomás and his brothers Domingo and Bernardo — were demanding an investigation into all the anonymous writings that were appearing. One of these was the *Observaciones sobre las Fábulas literarias originales de Don Tomás de Iriarte* (*Observations Concerning the Original Literary Fables of Don Tomás de Iriarte*), a pamphlet written by Félix María de Samaniego. Samaniego was angry because he had published a collection of literary fables in 1781, *after* submitting them to Iriarte for his comments, and Iriarte then claimed in 1782 to be the inventor of this fable form in Spanish.[5] While Iriarte was investigating the publication of the *Observations*, he ran across the *Grammarians* manuscript in Valencia. Forner had submitted the manuscript to Tomás de Orga, the publisher who had printed the second edition of *The Erudite Ass* after the Iriartes had gone all over Spain gathering up copies of the first edition and destroying them.[6]

If Forner had acted more discreetly, he probably would have managed to get *The Grammarians* printed. If the extraordinary viciousness of the satire is an indication of his anger, it is safe to assume that he was so blinded by vindictiveness that he did not consider the possibility that he would get caught. When Tomás de Iriarte found the manuscript, he and his brothers went before the appropriate authorities and demanded that the satire be confiscated and that Forner be forced to pay damages to the Iriarte family.

Forner replied to the charges in a legal statement sent to Count Floridablanca, but the council ruled against him. The manuscript was confiscated and a committee was sent to destroy all the remaining copies, but nothing was said about damages. Forner then sent another statement defending himself, this time to the king, but he received no reply.

During this crisis, one of the members of the council became convinced that Tomás de Iriarte was vain and cruel, and suggested to Floridablanca that Forner could use some help. The count offered to help him if he would promise to dedicate himself to more useful matters. Perhaps Forner promised to do so, but he continued satirizing Iriarte in his poetry until Iriarte's death in 1791. Iriarte never gave up either. His last poem — a sonnet dictated on his deathbed — attacked Forner. The manuscript of this sonnet in the National Library in Madrid has a note at the bottom supposedly in the hand of Don Bernardo de Iriarte: "To comment on this sonnet, I have begun a volume that will reach four thousand pages."[7]

CHAPTER 3

Masson's Attack on Spain and Forner's Apologetic Oration

I The Encyclopedia of Method: "What Do We Owe to Spain?"

THE work that brought Forner the greatest notoreity during his lifetime was the *Oración apologética por la España y su mérito literario (Apologetic Oration for Spain and Her Literary Merit)*, published in 1786. This, too, was a response to another author, and its publication was the culmination of a complicated series of events that began in 1783. That year was particularly important in the controversy between the Gallophiles and the Gallophobes in Spain. Forner had taken part in the controversy, as we have seen, through his attacks on Iriarte in *The Erudite Ass* and *The Grammarians*, both written in 1782. However, it was the publication in Paris of a dictionary of geography — a volume of the *Encyclopédie Méthodique (Encyclopedia of Method)* — that lead eventually to Forner's confirmation as the most important Gallophobe in Spain. The volume contained a long article on Spain written by Nicolás Masson de Morvilliers, a Frenchman who had devoted his life to studying geography and writing poetry. The article was an ignorant, insulting attack on Spain, and the Spaniards were furious.

Insofar as Masson deals with factual details about the regions, mountains, rivers, agriculture, economy, and history of Spain, the article is inoffensive. These objective data, however, are accompanied by extensive subjective material in which Masson analyzes the ills of the country as he sees them. He calls the Spaniards lethargic and indolent by nature, condemns their exploitation of the New World, and emphasizes the inefficiency of the government and the widespread ignorance of the general populace. Masson attributes almost all the country's defects to the influence of the church, which has turned the "colossal Spanish nation" into a "nation of pygmies.''[1] He suggests that the sparse population is due to two facts: that there is a celibate priest, monk, or nun for every thirty inhabitants, and that disabling diseases are rampant — smallpox among the young and syphilis among the adults of child-bearing age.

Masson attacks the Inquisition for its brutality and its censorship, and questions the power of a government in which "a king cannot make the slightest reform within the clergy of his kingdom without the permission of the sovereign in Rome."[2] Even when Masson says that his "impartiality" demands that he recognize the positive attributes of Spain, his affirmative comments are accompanied by anticlerical comments that serve to negate his evaluations: "The greater part of the universities are more richly endowed than those of France and England; but what kind of scholars can be produced by a country in which it is necessary to ask permission to think? . . . Where are their mathematicians, their physicists, their naturalists, their historians, and their philosophers?"[3]

Masson labels Spain "the most ignorant nation in Europe" and, by way of contrast, offers France as an example of an enlightened country. He then poses the question that would have extensive repercussions in Spain: "What do we owe to Spain? After two centuries, after four, after ten, what has she done for Europe?"[4]

II *The Replies to Masson*

These insulting remarks were nothing new, for similar things had already appeared in the writings of other eighteenth-century Frenchmen, such as Voltaire and Montesquieu.[5] But Masson's comments were particularly offensive because they seemed so out of place in an article on geography. The reactions to Masson's article took two different forms — direct rebuttals and indirect responses. The first two direct replies, curiously, had their origin outside Spain. In 1784, José Antonio de Cavanilles — an emminent Spanish priest and botanist living in Paris — published the *(Observations sur l'àrticle "Espagne" de la Nouvelle Encyclopédie (Observations Concerning the Article "Spain" in the New Encyclopedia)*. This book first appeared in Paris, and was then published in a Spanish translation by Mariano Rivera in Madrid in the same year. On January 26, 1786 Carlo Denina — an Italian living in Germany — delivered an address before the Berlin Academy, the "Réponse à la question: 'Que doit-on à l'Espagne?' " ("Reply to the Question 'What Do We Owe to Spain?' ''). It was Denina's address that eventually led to the publication of the *Apologetic Oration*, which Forner offered as the definitive reply to Masson.

The other kind of reply to Masson's article — the indirect response — proved to be much more significant in the history of Spanish literature. Masson's accusation that Spain had accomplished nothing and produced no outstanding men led the Spaniards to prove him wrong by presenting tangible evidence to the contrary. Two important examples of this kind of reaction — both begun in 1785 — were the *Theatro Hespañol (Spanish Theater)* of Vicente García de la Huerta, and the *Ensayo de una biblioteca española de los mejores escritores del reynado de Carlos III (Essay On a Spanish Library of the Best Writers of the Reign of Charles III)* of Juan Sempere y Guarinos. Huerta's *Spanish Theater* was a collection of seventeenth-century plays, and Sempere's *Library* was an encyclopedic work of hundreds of articles on writers of the second half of the eighteenth century. Both works were answers to Masson, and both were important in the career of Forner, who became involved in polemics as a result of their publication.

III   *Forner's* Letter from Don Antonio Varas

Although Forner's disputes with Huerta and Sempere were primarily concerned with the *Spanish Theater* and the *Library*, they began earlier, in 1784. In that year Forner published his *Carta de Don Antonio Varas al autor de "La riada" sobre la composición de este poema (Letter from Don Antonio Varas to the Author of "The Flood" About the Composition of This Poem)*. This was an attack on Cándido María Trigueros, the author of *La riada (The Flood)*, an epic poem about the disastrous floods along the Guadalquivir River in 1783 - 84. Trigueros was an older, established writer, commonly referred to as the "Philosopher Poet." Forner's *Letter from Varas* is somewhat temperate in its criticism, probably because of Trigueros' age and prestige, and because Forner had just emerged defeated from his polemic with Iriarte only two months before he published it. He assures Trigueros that he is not censuring the poet, but the poem, and only for the purpose of improving the state of poetry in Spain. For, "[the plague of bad poets] has reached such a point that several years ago a very learned and respectable body printed a semipolitical dialogue with the name of *Eclogue*, the style of which is at times comic, at times tragic, at times lyrical, at no time bucolic, and at all times ridiculous. . . . At the time, there was someone who proved this in a rather good discourse, which was not published, unfortunately for us."[6]

Of course, Forner is talking about Iriarte's eclogue. He is using the *Letter from Varas* to recall his feud with his old enemy and to compliment his own work, the *Comparison of the Eclogues*, in which he defended Meléndez Valdés. The Iriarte-Meléndez-Forner affair began to repeat itself only three days after these comments appeared in the *Letter from Varas*, with Trigueros as a sort of innocent bystander drawn into the dispute against his will. On July 16, as part of an elaborate celebration honoring the peace with France and the birth of twin sons to the royal family, two plays were presented for the first time — *Las bodas de Camacho (The Wedding of Camacho)* by Meléndez and *Los Menestrales (The Artisans)* by Trigueros. The two plays had won prizes in a competition whose judges included Gaspar Melchor de Jovellanos and Ignacio López de Ayala, both men of considerable stature as writers. On July 16, however, both plays were total disasters, although Meléndez' play — based on an episode in *Don Quixote* — was generally considered to be less ridiculous than Trigueros' *The Artisans*. The plays themselves fell into obscurity, but they were immediately immortalized in an epidemic of satirical verses that appeared all over Spain making great fun of the dramatic compositions.

One of the most famous at the time was a sonnet by Iriarte — "Oh, *Wedding of Camacho*, so wretched and rude/ . . . Oh, *Artisans*, insipidly wrought/ tavern-inspired . . . ."[7] A sonnet appeared in response to Iriarte's poem. This sonnet was attributed to Meléndez, but José Jurado recently suggested that it is in fact by Forner.

> "Apology Wrapped in Satire"
> Oh, poor don Tomás! Oh sad, sad muse,
> So luckless, so hapless, more frigid than frost!
> Oh *musical poem* too labored and lost!
> Brimming with languor, with sadness construed!
>   Oh, icy translation, insipidly wrought!
> Oh, tavernesque verses — oh, woe, woe is me!
> Oh talents of France, praisèd with glee
> Only by him who fine favors sought!
>   And though Cavanilles placed you ahead
> in excellence, naming you one of the blessed,
> You're still just a balladeer poet, so it's said.

And though you're so shameless, surpassing the rest
(Praise on, dear *Gaceta* until you are dead!)
Forner did the portrait that suited you best.

("*Apología envuelta en sátira*"
¡Oh pobre don Tomás! ¡Oh sin ventura
de triste numen más que el hielo helado!
¡Oh musical poema y malhadado!
¡Lleno de languidez y de tristura!
  ¡Oh fría traducción, insulsa dura!
¡Oh tabernario verso! ¡Ay me cuitado!
¡Oh talento francés solo alabado
de quien sólo favor lograr procura!
  Por más que Cavanilles por primero
te ponga y te publique gran poeta,
serás siempre poeta romancero.
  Y, aunque tu desvergüenza es bien completa,
Forner te hizo retrato verdadero,
y diga lo que quiera la Gaceta.)[8]

While there is no documentary proof that the sonnet is Forner's, it does sound like his satire. And it recalls many points of his polemic with Iriarte, brought up to date with references to Cavanilles — who praised Iriarte in the *Observations* — and to an article in the August 7, 1784 issue of the *Gaceta* that heaped lavish praise on Forner's enemy.

When the *Letter from Varas* appeared, Jovellanos took an active, though unobtrusive, part in the dispute. He wrote Trigueros a consoling letter, which he sent to the Philosopher Poet along with a copy of the Varas letter. Jovellanos hinted that the true author of the letter was Forner and that Forner had been reproached for his impious comments about the Royal Academy. Meanwhile, the Council of Castilla denounced the *Letter from Varas* and censured Forner. The academy initiated a decree against Forner, stating that he could satirize no one by name and publish nothing under a pseudonym. Thus, in a period of about six months, Forner had received two strong rebukes from the authorities — for *The Grammarians* and for the *Letter from Varas*. In a letter to a friend, Forner blamed the latest censure on Iriarte, Huerta, and López de Ayala, the censor who had approved the *Letter from Varas* for publication. According to Forner, when Ayala was called before the council to account for having approved the *Letter*, he claimed that Forner had not published it in the same form in which he had submitted it to the censor. Forner called that accusation ridiculous, and indicative of Ayala's lack of integrity.

IV   *Forner's* Spanish Captive Girl *and the* Letter to Ayala

Whether or not Ayala was telling the truth, the Varas episode had put him in an uncomfortable position, and Forner had acquired another enemy. Ayala soon had the opportunity to take revenge, when Forner requested official permission to publish his new play, *La cautiva española (The Spanish Captive Girl)*. Ayala, who was still the censor, rejected the play. Forner's response to this affront was his *Carta . . . a Don Ignacio López de Ayala . . . sobre haberle desaprobado su drama intitulado "La cautiva española" (Letter . . . to Don Ignacio López de Ayala . . . Concerning His Having Rejected the Drama Entitled "The Spanish Captive Girl")*.

This pamphlet is particularly interesting for two reasons: it brings up once again the presence of Masson's article in these disputes; and it is a good example of Forner's suddenly involving another writer in the fight. Forner claims in the *Letter to Ayala* that he wrote the play to prove Masson wrong, by showing that a Spaniard could produce good dramatic literature, and that Ayala worked against the good of his country in rejecting the play. He arrogantly proclaims that his play is better than all the trash that is presented every day on the stages of Spain, and that Ayala rejected it because it is so much better than his own plays. Forner then renders a vicious attack on a play by Ayala, *La Numancia*, saying that "the scene of Megara and the child, in such a turbulent and terrifying occasion, is totally improper; much like the phlegm that some assassins spout in a certain tragedy, inverisimilar to the highest degree, in the midst of such overwhelming struggles."[9] This "certain tragedy," which Forner does not name in the letter, is *Raquel*, the most famous play of García de la Huerta. Just as he did in the *Letter from Varas*, Forner has departed from the main purpose of his letter to strike out at someone else. This comment, then, broadens the scope of the polemic to include Huerta, who will have ample opportunity to respond when he publishes his *Spanish Theater*.

Forner continues the *Letter to Ayala* with more personal attacks, and ends up referring to him as Monsieur Ayala, which is just about the worst thing he could have called him at that time. He ends the letter by recalling Ayala's embarrassment over his last confrontation with Forner:

You gave an unjust censure, revealing the spirit of revenge that moved you; with which you fell into greater discredit than that which the assault of Antonio Varas was able to arouse in you. I think that you understand me; and meanwhile, best of luck! And be sure that your censure and your ratty vengeance, far from giving me displeasure, have granted me the opportunity to enjoy myself at your expense more than a couple of times with a number of friends.[10]

V   *Sempere's* Library of the Best Writers

Shortly after the *Letter to Ayala* appeared, Juan Sempere y Guarinos published the first volume of his *Library of the Best Writers*. This encyclopedia of literature, one of the monumental projects of the eighteenth century in Spain, eventually contained over fifteen hundred pages in six volumes. Sempere's preface to the first volume is another indication of the influence of Masson's article in Spain.

The publication of the *Encyclopedia of Method* and various conversations that I have heard about that work and about the *Observations* published in Paris by Don Antonio Cavanilles have made me much more aware of the need to inform the public more adequately about the present state of our literature. The apologia form is not sufficient for this [purpose]. . . . However well done they may be, these apologies always seem to be influenced excessively by patriotism, party spirit, etc., and for the most part simply complicate the issues with which they deal.[11]

In criticizing the apologies, Sempere is talking primarily about Cavanilles' *Observations*, the only one that had attracted much attention at that point. The comments that Sempere had heard about it were not good, for Cavanilles had defended Spain rather poorly, and had even suggested that Masson was right in saying that *contemporary* Spain lacked any significant literature. Sempere's *Library*, then, was an attempt to prove both Masson and Cavanilles wrong, by presenting several hundred commentaries on current writers. Although his encyclopedia turned out to be filled with many arbitrary evaluations motivated by the patriotism and party spirit for which he had criticized the apologies, it is invaluable as a source of information about Forner's contemporaries.

VI   *Forner's* Apologetic Oration

Sempere's negative comments about the apologia form made a lot of people angry, particularly Forner, who had just completed his *Apologetic Oration for Spain and Her Literary Merit*. Sempere probably did not know about it, since it was not yet in print, but Forner must have been offended by Sempere's questioning the validity and efficacy of the activity in which he was engaged. The Royal Academy of Language was equally sensitive to this criticism. In the same year, 1785, it had sponsored a competition for a rhetorical work — an apology in defense of Spain and her accomplishments in art and science. This contest was another response to the Masson article and similar attacks by other Frenchmen, but it was a failure. All the manuscripts submitted were judged unsuitable or unworthy of recognition, and the prize was not awarded. One of the rejected manuscripts was Forner's *Apologetic Oration*.

At this point, Forner was in an unstable position. He had attracted a great deal of attention, and had succeeded in linking his name with almost every prominent literary man in Spain — Iriarte, Huerta, Ayala, Trigueros, Meléndez, Jovellanos. Yet, he had managed to publish only two works of any significance, the *Satire Against the Vices Introduced Into Castilian Poetry* and *The Erudite Ass*. Other than these, and the letters to Trigueros and López de Ayala, he had only a series of disappointments to his credit — the unpublished *Comparison of the Eclogues*, the censured *Grammarians*, the rejected *Spanish Captive Girl*, and several other works for which he had found no publisher.

The academy's rejection of the *Apologetic Oration* was surely a bitter disappointment to Forner at that point in his life. Within a year, however, it was in print. The way in which Forner managed that is a good example of the persistence and ingenuity for which he was well known. On January 26, 1786, Carlo Denina delivered his Berlin Academy address responding to the Masson article. There was interest in publishing Denina's address in Spain, but since it was delivered in French, it had to be translated. Eugenio Llaguno, a high government official and member of the Academy of History, was a friend of Forner and gave him the task of translating the address. Forner hurriedly prepared the translation, and wrote Llaguno that they had to work fast, because "we are threatened with another translation of Denina, and I would not want to be left with all my work wasted and in vain."[12] When Forner sent the translation to Llaguno, he had included as a preface his own *Apologetic Oration*, which was fully twice as long as the Denina address. With his typical lack of modesty, Forner attached a letter in which he commented that the *Oration* "says everything that could be said, and in a new way."[13]

Llaguno sent the Denina address and the *Apologetic Oration* to Count Floridablanca for his approval, explaining what Forner had done. The count had already been involved in the reactions to the Masson article. When it first appeared in 1782, he sent notice of his displeasure to the French government through the Spanish ambassador. When Floridablanca received the two works from Llaguno, he replied with a letter telling him that Forner's *Oration* was "good" and authorizing the publication of the address along with Forner's preface. But he said that the Denina discourse should be printed in French, since "our defense must be made in that language which all nations read and understand, for in Spain we have a good idea of ourselves without needing this translation or the great apologies."[14]

Floridablanca's response is curiously contradictory. First, he is admitting that no one reads Spanish except the Spaniards, and that this defense of Spain should be made accessible to Europe, not to Spain alone. He indicates that the Spaniards have confidence in themselves and that all these apologies and defenses are wasted on them. The logical thing, then, would have been an edition in French of both Denina's address and Forner's apology. But, as it turned out, Denina appeared in French as a sort of appendix to Forner's *Apologetic Oration*, in Spanish, and Floridablanca even contributed six thousand reales toward the costs of publication. Forner's translation was discarded, but his work certainly was not "wasted and in vain." He had succeeded in getting his apology published, and he even included in the edition another work, the "Contestación al Discurso CXIII de *El Censor*" ("Answer to the Discourse CXIII of *The Censor*"), another attack on Iriarte, in response to an article in the newspaper *El Censor*.

The most remarkable thing about this episode is that Forner's *Oration* appeared in the same volume with Denina's discourse, for there were some comments in that address that Forner must have disagreed with vehemently. Denina's response to Masson is much more reasonable and intelligent than Cavanilles' *Observations*, which attempted to find a Spanish source for almost every achievement of Western culture. Denina offers a point-by-point rebuttal of Masson, and succeeds in showing that Spain has indeed contributed to the progress of Europe. But Denina tends to be sympathetic to the French; he ends his address by saying that only France has been worthy of Spain's attention during the last century, but that the political antipathy between the two nations has prevented Spain from benefitting from French cultural advances. These statements are the kind of Gallophile propaganda that always infuriated Forner, yet there is no criticism of Denina's ideas in the prologue that Forner added to the *Apologetic Oration* for the 1786 edition. This is truly an interesting moment in Forner's career, for it is the only time that he suppresses his own objections for the sake of expediency.

In his prologue Forner discusses the circumstances surrounding the publication of the book, and his version of the incident is not quite the same as that indicated by the documents of the period. He says that he first intended to publish Denina's address in Spanish, adding sarcastically that he "considered this necessary to understand it, since the language in which it is written is so vulgar. . . ."[15] But he changed his mind because of a suggestion, made by "a gentleman no less illustrious for his intelligence than for his tireless efforts for the good of our country," that it should be published in "the language that is generally understood throughout Europe." Forner then says that he was going to reprint Denina's discourse in the original French, except for "the chance occurrence that some intelligent men gave their approval to an *Oration* that I had written a little while ago in defense of our literature, only for the purpose of exercising my style in Castilian eloquence."[16]

Thus, after submitting the *Oration* to the academy, and after having it rejected, Forner audaciously claims that he wrote it only as a pastime, and published it only because of "the favorable votes with which the persons to whom I had entrusted it privately returned it."[17] It is worth pointing out that these comments come *after* Forner had engaged in those bitter exchanges with Iriarte, after he had made a name for himself throughout Spain as an arrogant, outspoken critic of anyone with whom he disagreed. This prologue, with its adulation of Floridablanca and its self-adulation, is perhaps the work that reveals Forner's personality most clearly.

Near the end of the prologue, Forner sets forth the purpose of his *Apologetic Oration*: "to demonstrate the merit of learning in Spain through the utility of the subjects to which the learned Spaniards have consecrated the application of their knowledge."[18] This is an important statement, for it is a concise expression of the theme of the apology — the utility of the subjects. While Cavanilles and Denina had tried to show that Spain did indeed have those scientists and philosophers that Masson did not find in Spain, Forner discounts the value of science and philosophy, unless it is "useful" and "utilitarian." He says very clearly that science is useless for explaining the world, because only "revealed truth" can do that. Although the title of Forner's work indicates that it deals with the literary merit of Spain, the *Oration* has very little to do with literature. It deals almost entirely with philosophy, and its main point is that only the "utilitarian" philosophers are worthy of study. What Forner means by "utilitarian" coincides with the ideas of Andrés Piquer in his article on censorship: philosophy is "useful" so long as it contributes to human happiness, so long as it is to the glory of God and beneficial to man's well-being in the context of society.

Forner's *Apologetic Oration* is obviously anti-intellectual in its attitude, for it is a fierce defense of tradition and "revealed truth." Spain, according to Forner, is the nation that has always excelled in the preservation of that revealed truth. France, on the other hand, by seeking to undermine the validity of this useful knowledge, has only contributed to man's unhappiness.

The *Oration* takes such a strong position in favor of the traditional values of church and state that it is not surprising that it elicited a host of negative responses. But, before they began to appear, Forner became involved once again in a dispute with Vicente García de la Huerta.

VII *Huerta's* Spanish Theater

In 1785, the year before the appearance of Forner's *Oration*, Huerta had published the first volume of the *Spanish Theater*. In a two hundred page prologue, he responded to Masson with an impassioned defense of the Spanish drama of the sixteenth and seventeenth centuries. The purpose of the *Spanish Theater*, according to Huerta, was to make available in correct, uncontaminated editions the best plays of the seventeenth century and to correct the false notions conveyed by foreign critics who had denigrated Spanish dramatic literature and published inaccurate translations of the plays. He was defending the Spanish drama primarily to "inform the general public of Europe, where the malicious have spread their calumnies, and the stupid and ill-informed their gross errors."[19]

In theory Huerta's *Spanish Theater* is an admirable response to Masson, for it offers the literature itself rather than simply a polemical defense without evidence. However, this potentially significant approach is undermined by Huerta's own concept of theater. He was a dramatist of neoclassic orientation and he constantly has to apologize for the blatant irregularity of seventeenth-century drama and its lack of adherence to the most elementary precepts of "good theater" from the neoclassic point of view. He tries to compensate for these "defects" by emphasizing the remarkable inspiration and ingenuity of the plays, but this results in a rather weak argument since the French critics like Masson had attacked the plays precisely on the grounds of lack of discipline.

Also, when Huerta compiled his collection he concentrated on certain types of plays, mainly *comedias de figurón* (caricature plays) and *comedias de capa y espada* (cape and sword plays). As Cotarelo points out, "Huerta ruined his eyes looking for the very thing that does not exist in our theater: characterization and moral end."[20] As a result, the collection did not include the really outstanding plays, because those plays could in no way be considered neoclassic. In seventeen volumes he included a total of only thirty-six plays, and of those, only about six or seven would be considered today as important to an understanding of the seventeenth-century Spanish drama. Thus, as a representative selection designed to prove the excellence of the theater in Spain, Huerta's collection was largely a failure.

Huerta's prologue is equally unsuccessful, for it is almost as absurd as the writings of the French critics. Rather than analyze their criticisms to show where they are wrong, he spends most of his time pointing out the inadequacies of French theater and the stupidity of the critics themselves. The prologue is made even more ridiculous by a peculiar orthography that reached hilarious proportions. The title — *Theatro Hespañol*, rather than the current form, *Teatro Español* — is an example, and Huerta goes so far as to render *Sevilla* as *Sebilla, bulto* as *vulto, sátira* as *sátyra, filósofo* as *philósopho*. This unusual spelling is accompanied by numerous neologisms — most of them inventions of Huerta himself — that subsequently were satirized extensively in the replies to the *Spanish Theater*. And there were many responses, because Huerta's fellow countrymen were incensed by a negative presentation of Cervantes in the prologue and by veiled references to those Spanish critics who "never create anything of their own and always find the labors of others defective" and whose principal motives are "stupidity, whim, and most often, envy."[21] Huerta did not name Forner as one of those critics, but the description fits him perfectly, except that Forner was not stupid. And because he was not stupid, he surely knew that Huerta was directing this statement at him. It is safe to assume that Huerta had not forgotten the *Letter to Ayala* and its reference to *Raquel*.

VIII *Attacks on the* Spanish Theater

Forner did not respond to Huerta until later, probably because he was involved in the *Apologetic Oration* project at the time that the *Spanish Theater* appeared. The first answer to Huerta's comments was an anonymous publication, the *Continuación de las memorias críticas de Cosme Damián (Continuation of the Critical Memoirs of Cosme Damián)*. The author was Félix María de Samaniego, the fabulist and enemy of Iriarte. In the *Critical Memoirs*, Samaniego makes great fun of Huerta's orthography and of his neologisms, particularly *transpirenaica* ("transpyrenaic"), a term invented by Huerta to refer to anything on the other side of the Pyrenees. Samaniego points out that Huerta has undertaken an enormous task which has been attempted and abandoned by several writers before, but that "a vehement and sublime talent, a vast and exquisite erudition, a righteous and *dispreoccupied* judgment, together with the most fortunate boldness in the world, led him [Huerta] to embrace such a gigantic task and to find it quite inferior to his strengths."[22]

To counter Huerta's criticism of Cervantes, Samaniego prefaces the *Memoirs* with an epigraph, a quotation from the *Quixote:* ". . . because foreigners, who very strictly observe the rules of the comedia, hold us to be barbarian and ignorant, seeing the absurd and ridiculous things in the plays that we write. *Quix. p. 1, c. xlvii.*"[23] Huerta had claimed that the negative attitudes toward the Spanish dramatists were the result of "transpyrenaic frivolity." Samaniego answers by citing a similar attitude found in the masterwork of Spanish literature. Then, with evident sarcasm, he asks why Huerta did not combat those negative opinions by choosing plays that do conform to the eighteenth-century idea of what theater should be. The answer is obvious: because there are none. So, if there are none why did he not simply rewrite them to conform to the precepts of neoclassic theater? Samaniego's suggestion is not as outrageous as it seems, for this is precisely what had been done by several dramatists, including Trigueros, López de Ayala, and Tomás Sebastián y Latre. Samaniego then confesses that "if the writer of these *Memoirs* . . . possessed the dramatic knowledge of the author of *Raquel*, he would not cede to the good professor Ayala, nor to anyone else, the glory of compiling a theater which, corrected, would be infinitely superior in its comic aspects to any that are now known."[24]

Huerta responded immediately with a work that drew Forner into this polemic, the *Lección crítica a los lectores del papel intitulado*

"Continuación de las memorias críticas de Cosme Damián" (*Lesson in Criticism to the Readers of the Paper Entitled "Continuation of the Critical Memoirs of Cosme Damián"*). Huerta begins by saying that the only thing worth reading in the *Memoirs* is the quotation from Cervantes, and that even that is inaccurate. Samaniego has erred in his documentation, for the passage is from chapter forty-eight of the first part of the *Quixote*, not from chapter forty-seven And Cervantes erred in his observation, because at the time that he said it, there were no other nations with a theater that followed the precepts. And even if it were true, the reference is meaningless, because Huerta was not defending the Spanish theater from the defects that Cervantes was talking about. Furthermore, not a single play included in the *Spanish Theater* had been written at the time that Cervantes wrote that criticism in the *Quixote*. Huerta then augments his earlier criticism of Cervantes, saying that "the most absurd, ridiculous, and abominable of all [the Spanish plays] are those written by Cervantes"[25] and that Cervantes wrote them only because he was jealous of Lope de Vega.

In a footnote to his comments about Cervantes, Huerta tells a story in response to Forner's comments about *Raquel* in the *Letter to Ayala*.

A one-eyed fellow was adding some notes to a certain modern tragedy, the author of which had put him in a bad mood because of the applause that he had received. He came to a passage in which — so he thought — certain villains were spending too much time talking, and were not killing the victim as quickly as he would have liked. So he put the following note, or something like it: "These assassins are wasting too much phlegm." A friend of his — with better judgment and more dispreoccupied — saw him by chance and, reflecting on the situation, told him: "But, my friend, this note is not appropriate, because these are not assassins." To which he replied: "That is true, my friend; but since I am one-eyed, I usually do not see things straight; and finally, in order to find something to say, I have to get things mixed up to make trouble." To be sure, there is always some troublemaker with one eye (or with two) waiting around for a chance to make criticisms even against the will of Minerva herself.[26]

IX   *Forner and Tomé Cecial*

The effect of this story in Huerta's *Lesson in Criticism* was far-reaching. The term *tuerto* (one-eyed) immediately became a kind of catchword for Forner in the newspapers and periodicals of the day. Forner himself did a great deal toward making himself the object of

many *tuerto* jokes by intensifying this polemic with a bitter reply —
the *Reflexiones sobre la "Lección crítica" que ha publicado Don
Vicente García de la Huerta: las escribía en vindicación de la buena
memoria de Miguel de Cervantes Saavedra Tomé Cecial, ex-
escudero del bachiller Sansón Carrasco* (*Reflections Concerning The
"Lesson in Criticism" Published by Don Vicente García de la Huerta: Written in Vindication of the Good Memory of Miguel de Cervantes Saavedra by Tomé Cecial, Ex-Squire of the Graduate Sansón
Carrasco*). This pamphlet was an answer to Huerta's criticism of Cervantes and, quite appropriately, Forner chose as his pseudonym
Tomé Cecial, the squire of Sansón Carrasco in Cervantes' *Don Quixote*.

The *Reflections of Tomé Cecial* is more important than many of
Forner's polemical pamphlets, because he deals specifically with the
ideas expressed in the work that he is attacking rather than simply
satirizing the writer of that work. However, as he defends Cervantes
as a playwright who really tried to follow the precepts of the drama
and thus reform the theater of Spain, Forner does not refrain from
making many unattractive comments about Huerta himself. He calls
the "one-eyed" story in the *Lesson in Criticism* an "absurd fiction
that could have existed only in the person who invented it"[27] and
says that if his eloquence matched Huerta's, he would observe that
"without his grace's being *one-eyed* or *myopic*, he sees things
backward, or in a way quite different from everyone else . . . and
this is no doubt a case of his comprehension's surely not seeing very
much straight ahead."[28] As he quotes from the *Lesson in Criticism*,
he begs his readers to "have the good grace to pardon me for the
boredom that I am going to cause them by making them read this"[29]
and he claims to have a collection of Huerta's poetry, which he keeps
close at hand "for when I am sad and in need of a good laugh."[30]
Then, after all this sarcastic invective against the "unfortunate"
author of the *Spanish Theater*, Forner assures the reader that
"criticism many times is charity, as it was in Cervantes, and as it is at
the present moment in me."[31]

Obviously, Huerta did not think that Forner's criticism was
charitable, and he replied to the *Reflections* with *La Escena
Hespañola defendida en el "Prólogo" del "Theatro Hespañol" de D.
Vicente García de la Huerta y en su "Lección crítica"* (*The Spanish
Stage Defended in the "Prologue" to the "Spanish Theater" of Don
Vicente García de la Huerta and in his "Lesson in Criticism"*). This
was a reprint of the prologue to the *Spanish Theater* with about a

dozen notes added "to give more clarity to certain passages which, because of pure moderation on my part, did not include everything that, afterward, has become necessary."[32] Rather than simply clarifications, Huerta's additional notes are really answers to Forner's comments about the first edition of the prologue. He intensifies his anti-Cervantine position, accusing Cervantes of pride, envy, and arrogance. He praises Cavanilles — who had praised Huerta in the *Observations* — for having "shut the mouth of those who are envious of the merit of the Spaniards, at least for now."[33] Huerta then even accuses Forner of imitating the French critics of Spanish literature: "the ridiculous absolute statements of the French critics have been imitated by some of our modern critics. The ingenious editor of the *Reflections of Tomé Cecial* says, speaking of my eclogue entitled *The Bereberes*, that *it is a Ballading-dong exchanged between some Moorons [un Romanzón entre unos Morazos]*."[34] He also recalls in detail one of Forner's less pleasant memories, the rejection of *The Spanish Captive Girl*.

A certain critic, after writing a satire against idiotic comedias, tried to do one himself, and it came out so idiotic . . . that the actors refused to produce it and the censor refused to approve it, because of the very absurdities for which the actors had rejected it. . . . With all this it is necessary to concede to this critic his sufficient ability in other matters of more gravity, in which he has made some singular and notorious contributions. Take a look at the story of the one-eyed man who added notes to a certain tragedy etc. etc. *Lesson in Criticism*, pag. XLVIII [*sic* for XLIII].[35]

Huerta ends the reprint of the prologue with a note suggesting that critics like Forner should be called "criticanines" because of "their cacopho-nasty mania and their habit of biting and barking at every living thing," and that Forner's stupid *Reflections* is written in "the manner of composing pamphlets typical of those people who cannot manage to do anything else."[36]

Since Forner was not one to let his enemy have the last word, he responded to Huerta with a *Fe de erratas del "Prólogo" del "Theatro Hespañol" (List of Errata for the "Prologue" of the "Spanish Theater")*. This pamphlet is one of Forner's most ingenious polemical works. He approaches the new prologue-with-notes from the point of view of a proofreader correcting what must be erroneous interpolations of the printer, since even Huerta cannot be stupid enough to write such incomprehensible absurdities. Forner suggests that this *List of Errata* be put at the beginning of the prologue as a kind of "supplement," and that the reader

mark out everything from the first page through page CCVI, everything from the words *My brother Don Pedro* to the word *patriotism* [the first and last words of the prologue] and put in its place another prologue written in a pure language. Since they speak *gibberish* all over the world, and the lucid theaterist destined his *Prologue* to be read by all nations in the place of the *Quixote*, no doubt he felt it advantageous to use a language that would be understood everywhere, except in Spain.[37]

Forner then presents a sarcastic comparison of the prologue and the *Quixote* to prove that while Cervantes' masterpiece is puerile, insipid, and the result of the author's envy, Huerta's prologue is elegant, refined, and august to such an extent that even a blind man could see the difference between the two. In the course of all this diatribe, Forner does make some serious observations. He emphasizes the point that the Spaniards should not "increase their self-deception by praising the vain inclination to prefer our own things — just because they are ours — over reason, good taste, and truth."[38] The *Quixote*, then, should not be praised just because it is Spanish, but because of its intrinsic value as literature. Of course, this comment also has its satirical intent: neither should the prologue to the *Spanish Theater* be accepted just because it is Spanish; rather, it should be judged on its merit, of which it has none.

Huerta's *Spanish Theater* became the subject of parodies written by several authors other than Forner, and the Huerta-Forner dispute was the source of many satirical treatments in the poetry of their contemporaries. Jovellanos wrote a long ballad about their polemic, in which Huerta succeeds in leaving Forner "one-eyed for the rest of his life."[39] Forner, smarting from this insult, rewrote Jovellanos' ballad with a new second part which changed the poem into a dispute between Huerta and Iriarte. Later, Jovellanos accused Forner of plagiarism, saying that he had incorporated the first part of the Jovellanos ballad into the poem, calling it his own.

Most of these attacks on the author of the *Spanish Theater* ended when Huerta died on March 12, 1787. Forner, however, did not let his adversary's death stand in his way. He wrote a poem, "El Morión," probably after Huerta's demise. This poem is addressed to Madness, which Forner says is Huerta's only muse, and includes intact the first line of the *First Solitude* by Góngora: " 'Twas of the

year the flowered season.''[40] Forner surely incorporates this line into
the poem to reinforce his image of Huerta as a blabbering idiot
capable of writing nothing but rubbish akin to the most corrupt and
extravagant poetry of Góngora. The theme of Huerta's insanity is
repeated in a poem dedicated to him after his death by Iriarte, with a
reference to the famous madhouse in Zaragossa.

> Of judgment, but not of genius deplete,
> Huerta the audacious here enjoys his rest;
> Parnassus is left with a vacant seat,
> And the cages of Zaragossa have lost a guest.
> (*De juicio sí, mas no de ingenio escaso,
> aquí, Huerta el audaz, descanso goza:
> deja un puesto vacante en el Parnaso
> y una jaula vacía en Zaragoza.*)[41]

Whether the madhouse lost an inmate with Huerta's death
depends, of course, on one's opinion of his literary activities. Forner,
however, certainly lost a valuable enemy, for it was in the exchanges
with Huerta that he reached his zenith as a satirist. But Forner was
not without further material for his polemical bent. At about the
same time that Huerta died, the responses to the *Apologetic Oration*
began to appear.

X   *The Attacks on the* Apologetic Oration

One of the more substantial attacks on the *Oration* was the *Carta
al autor de la "Oración apologética por la España y su mérito
literario" (Letter to the Author of the "Apologetic Oration for Spain
and her Literary Merit")*, published in 1787 under the pseudonymn
Josef Conchudo. The true authorship of this pamphlet has never
been determined, although many critics have suggested that it was
written by Iriarte. Conchudo, whoever he was in reality, primarily
censures Forner's deprecatory comments about natural science, ask-
ing repeatedly if it was necessary "to scorn the sciences in which we
have not flowered as much as other nations" in order to write a simple historical discourse about Spain's contributions.[42] Conchudo is
correct in his observation: Forner does tend to scorn any kind of
achievement by other countries if Spain has not been outstanding in
that particular area. Throughout his career, Forner takes this attitude: if Spain has not done it, it is not worth doing.

As Conchudo criticizes Forner's ideas, he satirizes the style of the
Apologetic Oration, particularly Forner's reference to moral

philosophy — ethics — as the "*noble branch of philosophy.*" Conchudo's purpose in writing the *Letter* is "to note how strange it is that you treat poorly some outstanding foreign philosophers to whom we owe almost all our knowledge about mathematics and natural sciences, and to show that you have proceeded in this with as much levity as M. Masson in his stupid question [What has Spain done...?], in order that the means by which you set forth the advancement of this *noble branch of philosophy* should not be undermined, for sometimes a gross tract has more influence than one thinks ...."[43]

Conchudo excuses himself from analyzing the *Oration*, saying that Forner would have to express himself much more clearly for him to be able to do that. He points out in particular Forner's confused scorn of Newton, and suggests that Forner has not even read the works of Newton or that if he has, he has not understood the first thing about that scientist's discoveries and theories. Unfortunately, Forner is one of that decreasing number of men who "believe that the happiness of the human species consists only of reading the Christian canon and knowing how to interpret a Roman law."[44]

There was also a series of attacks on the *Oration* in the newspapers, such as *The Universal Apologist* and *The Censor*, the journal that Forner attacked in the appendix to the *Oration*. One of the *Apologist* articles was even reprinted in another periodical, the *Correo de Madrid (Madrid Dispatch)*.

Letter. I have received the ridiculous apology of Forner .... To tell the truth, I do not understand it, nor do I believe that there is anyone in the world who does, except Forner himself.... The worst thing I find in it: this business of making the sciences ridiculous is the most ridiculous thing imaginable.... To his malice he adds hypocrisy in what he writes to *The Censor*, which doubtless will remain silent, but will not be convinced. All in all, and taking ill for ill, I think that the apology of Cavanilles is better.[45]

In an earlier number, the *Apologist* had printed another article on the *Oration*, which analyzed Forner's work by organizing his statements into categories labeled chards, cabbages, black beans, carrots, lentils, etc.[46]

XI Forner's Response

In that same year — 1787 — Forner responded to these journalistic attacks with several works. The first was the *Conversaciones familiares entre "El Censor," "El Apologista Universal," y un doctor en leyes: en las cuales se procura hacer el panegírico de aquellos dos grandes maestros de nuestra nación, y se da a conocer el mérito de sus imortales escritos (Intimate Conversations Between "The Censor," "The Universal Apologist," and a Doctor of Law: In Which There Is Attempted a Panegyric of Those Two Great Teachers of Our Nation, and In Which Is Made Known the Merit of Their Immortal Writings).* These "intimate conversations" — published under the pseudonym Silvio Liberio — depict a whole group of Forner's "learned enemies" gathered around the dinner table, speaking the most incredible commonplaces as if they were divine words of wisdom. They suggest that *The Censor, The Apologist,* and the *Literary Digest* form a kind of literary guitar, the three forming the keys, the strings, and the body. They get into a fierce argument about which could best be the body, each claiming that he is more hollow than the others.[47] Forner suggests that all these conversations should be recorded by Sempere to use as a supplement to his "exacting and supremely useful *Library.*"[48]

About the same time, Forner published another similar pamphlet, the *Demostraciónes palmarias (Clear Demonstrations),* under the pseudonymn Regañadientes (Tooth-Gnasher).[49] In response to this, *The Censor* printed a parody entitled "Oración apologética por el Africa y su mérito literario ("Apologetic Oration for Africa and Her Literary Merit"), which opens with the "simplistic" first line of Forner's *Oration:*"The scientific glory of a nation should not be measured by its advances in superfluous or prejudicial things." And soon afterward *The Universal Apologist* published a thirty-two page article devoted to proving beyond any doubt that Forner was a fake and a charlatan.[50] Forner replied with the *Pasatiempo de D. Juan Pablo Forner en respuesta a las objeciones que se han hecho a su "Oración apologética por la España" (Pastime of Don Juan Pablo Forner in Reply To the Objections That Have Been Made to the "Apologetic Oration for Spain").* Taking his cue from the Cave of Montesinos episode in the *Quixote* (Part II, Chapter 23), Forner includes a letter from Tomé Cecial, written from the Elysian Fields, telling Forner about the great fun made of the *Apologist* attack by the devils themselves.

In the midst of all these insults and counterinsults, Forner wrote his response to the Conchudo letter, the *Antisofisma, o sea, desenredo de los sofismas con que se ha pretendido obscurecer algunas doctrinas de la "Oración apologética por la España y su mérito literario" de D. Juan Pablo Forner, por E. C. V. (An-*

*tisophistry, Or Rather, An Unraveling of the Sophistries With Which
They Have Tried to Obscure Some Of the Doctrines Of the
"Apologetic Oration For Spain and Her Literary Merit" of Don Juan
Pablo Forner, by E. C. V.).* The *Antisophistry* reveals that the
Conchudo epistle really hurt Forner's pride, and that he was most
offended by the suggestion that he had not read or understood the
work of Newton. He spends a lot of time carefully explaining Newton's system of the planets, surely for no other reason than to prove
that he has indeed read it. He insists that he did not discount the advances of science; rather, he only criticized the current tendency to
think that science provides all the answers — "the hyperbolic air
with which the modern-maniacs try to illuminate us."[51] Forner
defends himself by suggesting that Conchudo has not understood
that someone could read Newton and still not "subject his neck to
the yoke of Newtonism, for . . . according to this new principle of the
Newtonian Conchudo, either we will not open the works of the
English philosopher and thus be whimsical and ignorant critics, or
else, faithful sectarians of gravitational pull, we will walk around
with the *prism* in hand through the immensity of the *void*, scorning
as idiotic all those that do not include themselves in this
philosophical procession."[52]

Forner ends the *Antisophistry* with an ironic concession to
Conchudo's interest in acknowledging the advances of science by
saying that "it is, of course, true that physics has a certain attraction
of splendor, of adornment, brilliance, beauty, *nobility*, and *eclat*
—this last one in order to express myself *transpyrenaically*."[53] This
last comment suggests that Forner suspected that Huerta had
written the *Letter to the Author of the "Apologetic Oration."* Or
perhaps he alluded to the unusual language of the *Spanish Theater*
prologue to insinuate that Conchudo was as ridiculous as Huerta.

The following year — 1788 — another assault on the *Oration*
appeared, the *Cartas de un español residente en París a su hermano
residente en Madrid sobre la "Oración apologética por la España y
su mérito literario," de D. Juan Pablo Forner (Letters from a
Spaniard Living in Paris to His Brother Living in Madrid Concerning the "Apologetic Oration . . .").* At the time many attributed this
to Iriarte, but Forner thought that it was from the pen of Antonio
Borrego, whom Cotarelo identifies tentatively as the brother of
Tomás Borrego, the author of a *Universal History* that Forner had
criticized.[54] The pamphlet makes fun of Forner's use of language in
the *Oration* and also attacks Cervantes: "Either Don Quixote

destroyed the chivalric spirit that affected the nobility, or he did not. If he did not, we owe nothing to Cervantes except his having entertained us, in spite of what Forner says. If he did destroy it, what virtues or vices have filled the void left by that spirit?"[55]

This was a serious criticism in the eighteenth century, so caught up in the spirit of *utile dulci* — the concept that art should instruct as it entertains. The suggestion that the *Quixote* did no more than amuse evoked a quick response from Forner, the *Lista puntual de los errores, equivocaciones, sofismas, e impertinencias de que está atiborrada la primera carta de las que el español ha escrito contra la "Oración apologética"* (*Punctual List of the Errors, Mistakes, Sophistries, and Impertinences Stuffed Into the First of the Letters Written By the Spaniard Against the "Apologetic Oration"*). This work is just what its title says — a list of the Spaniard's misconceptions about Forner's defense of Spain against the Masson article. He discredits the *Letters From a Spaniard* in a typical Fornerian fashion, addressing the prologue to the "idiotic reader" who cannot distinguish for himself the writings of sound critics from those of hodge-podge commentators. The *Punctual List* is not for the learned readers who can see these errors without Forner's assistance.[56]

The *Punctual List* was the last polemical work directly associated with the *Apologetic Oration*. Forner was a prolific polemist and he probably could have continued these attacks and counterattacks indefinitely, but he turned to other disputes, some with old enemies and some with new ones.

CHAPTER 4

Further Polemics:
Trigueros and Sempere

I *Trigueros and Forner's* Philosophical Discourses

EVEN in a period as replete with polemics as the eighteenth century, the extensiveness of the disputes occasioned by Masson's criticism is somewhat surprising. Although Forner's *Apologetic Oration* elicited no more attacks after about 1788, almost all of his subsequent literary conflicts were in some way related to the article in the *Encyclopedia of Method*.

Trigueros had not forgotten the *Letter from Antonio Varas* and renewed his animosity with Forner in 1789. Jovellanos, accustomed to offering sound advice to everyone, had encouraged Trigueros to stop writing poetry and "work on the other projects (*Memoirs for the History of Commerce in Bética*, etc.) in which you will have fewer envious ones [pursuing you], for perhaps there is no one who will presume to have the capacity to compete with you [in those fields]."[1] Trigueros ignored this advice, and published a poem, *Las majas* (*The Majas*), in 1789 as part of an elaborate celebration honoring the coronation of Charles IV. In the poem, Trigueros made a comment to the effect that Forner had thrown into the *Philosophical Discourses* "poor doctrine cast in poorer verses."[2]

Back in 1786, Forner published his *Discursos filosóficos sobre el hombre (Philosophical Discourses Concerning Man)*, a long poem written about 1780 and styled after Pope's *Essay on Man*. The *Discourses* were accompanied by hundreds of pages of notes in which Forner expanded and commented on the ideas presented in the verses, the same ideas that he later expressed in the *Apologetic Oration* and in the *Antisophistry*. In his self-defense to Floridablanca during the *Grammarians* affair, Forner used the poem as ammunition against Iriarte:

At the age of twenty-four I wrote five *Philosophical Discourses*, adjusted to the meter of poetry, impugning the sophisms of impiety and establishing the truths that touch on the nature of man. I had resolved to bring them to the public with the name of Your Excellency stamped on the front of them, with no purpose other than to make foreigners understand that under the ministry of Your Excellency Spain has provided a situation in which a young man can do what old men do in other nations. . . . Thus, the cultured nations would see . . . what has not been seen until now in our country. That is, philosophical subjects adjusted to meter, and a young man achieving what Alexander Pope did not achieve until a little before his death.[3]

Forner's flattery only made Floridablanca wary, and the count suspended the permission to publish *The Grammarians* until he could find out something about the personal qualities of Forner. The result was that *The Grammarians* was banned, and the *Philosophical Discourses* endured the censor's scrutiny for two years before they were finally published in 1786. When they did appear, there were several satirical responses. One appeared in 1788, the *Centones fornerianos: discurso antisofístico extractado del "Hombre" de Forner y traducido al quákaro (Fornerian Centones: Antisophistic Discourse Extracted From Forner's "Man" and Translated to the Quaker Tongue)*, which was published under the pseudonym M. Fox Novel and is attributed by Jiménez Salas to Iriarte.[4]

The cleverest commentary on the *Philosophical Discourses* was the *Apéndice a la primera salida de Don Quixote el escolástico (Appendix to the First Sally of Don Quixote the Scholastic)*, which appeared in 1789 under the pseudonym Eugenio Habela Patiño. This was an attack on both Forner's *Discourses* and the *Philosophical Compendium* of Roselli. Forner never responded directly to the *Appendix*, and this is surprising, for it said some terrible things. There is one section in which passages from Forner's poetry are compared with sections from Góngora's *Solitudes* to show that the only difference is that the syntactical transpositions are a little more frequent, violent, and disruptive in Góngora than in Forner. There is one very amusing passage in which a poet and a captain are discussing the efficacy (or usefulness) of Forner's verses:

"As a grammarian, philosopher, poet, and gentleman, I swear that I saw with my own eyes what I am going to say: I saw a man with insomnia, to whom the physicians had applied all the remedies they knew, without success. Then, since the poor fellow had asked for a book, luckily for him they brought him the *Philosophical Discourses*. He began to flip through the pages reading a verse here, a verse there; and, miracle of miracles, in an instant he was snoring away."

"According to that," said the captain, "whoever said it was not lying when he said that there is no book so bad that it does not have something good about it."[5]

II   *Sempere and Trigueros*

Forner's reply to these insulting commentaries was limited to a few references to them in the *Funeral Rite* and in one or two pamphlets. Forner also responded to Trigueros' comment in *The Majas* in the context of a more extensive attack on the just-published sixth volume of Juan Sempere y Guarinos' *Library of the Best Writers*, which included a forty-six page article on Trigueros. The article defends the Philosopher Poet (Trigueros) by presenting documentary proof that he is a good poet, whatever Forner may say.

At the same time that Mr. Masson was writing the article . . . which would scandalize the Spaniards so, another judicious French official, . . . in the midst of the delights of retirement, [was] reading works of ingenuity. Surprised at the ingenuity that he divined in some Spanish works, and particularly in the work of Señor Trigueros, . . . [he] wrote to Señor Vázquez, a bookseller in Seville. . . . Pondering the immense pleasure that its reading had caused him, and putting the work of the Philosophical Poet ahead of the best that the English and the French had written in this genre, he asked for a collection of Spanish authors with which to enrich his library.[6]

Sempere then includes a series of letters from this judicious Frenchman — Mr. D'Essars — and an anonymous ode written in the same hand, filled with adulatory comments on the work of Trigueros. This is all rather curious, for even Sempere must have known that Trigueros was not a very good poet. Most likely, the real intent of the article was to provide a rebuttal of Masson. The author of that infamous encyclopedia article was not the only Frenchman in the land, and here were letters from a Frenchman who had praised Spanish literature. Trigueros was the poet that Mr. D'Essars chose to praise, so Trigueros got more critical acclaim than he deserved in the course of Sempere's refutation of Masson's insults.

As Sempere discusses *The Flood*, he recalls the *Letter from Antonio Varas* and its "poorly applied commonplace comments, and certain expressions of Señor Trigueros misunderstood and maliciously glossed," as well as "the satisfaction that [Forner] was ordered to give before the Spanish Academy."[7] Sempere then

reprints a letter to Trigueros from Florian. The French fabulist
points out the "supreme sensibility" of *The Flood* and encourages
Trigueros to ignore all those vile satirists like Don Juan Pablo
Forner, for "Parnassus has always been infested with buzzards and
owls that make war on the nightingales."[8] The article ends with a
commentary on the obvious faults and shortcomings of Trigueros'
poems, which Sempere attributes to their having been written for
the occasion, hurriedly, and without the necessary polish. But in
spite of these weaknesses, Trigueros "will be reputed as one of our
greatest learned men, when time and enlightenment erase the im-
pressions that envy and malediction have propagated against [his
works]."[9]

It would be difficult to imagine a more contradictory article.
Sempere heaps lavish praise on Trigueros at one point, and then admits that his poetry and plays are not very good. To some extent, the
need to refute Masson explains Sempere's attitude toward both
Trigueros and Forner. If Sempere wanted to defend Trigueros in
order to prove Masson wrong, then it was natural that he censure
Forner's attack on *The Flood*. In a sense, Forner was caught in the
middle of this dispute between Sempere and Masson. Of course, it
would be absurd to think of Forner as an innocent bystander. He had
set himself up for all this, as he did throughout his career. And as
always, he was furious, particularly at the letter from Florian. He
wrote to Florian, and the fabulist replied with an apology and an explanation. He said that the letter reprinted in the article was in
response to a letter from Trigueros — whom he did not know — ask-
ing for comments about *The Flood* and the *Letter from Antonio
Varas*.

The Trigueros article was not the only thing in this sixth volume of
Sempere's *Library* to elicit the wrath of Forner. There is, for example, an article on Tomás de Iriarte which notes "his genius, his fecund numen and notable talents, . . . his elegant poetic works, his
taste and knowledge in music, his intelligence in different
languages, his criticism and his literature," and censures the
"atrocious and gross satires with which some have tried to defame
him."[10] Of these satires, Sempere singles out for extensive comment
the work that launched Forner's career.

Señor Forner, under the name of D. Pablo Segarra, published the paper
entitled *The Erudite Ass,* directed toward ridiculing and subjecting to scorn
the person and the writings of D. Tomás de Iriarte. . . . D. Pablo Segarra —

transformed now into Antonio Varas, now into Silvio Liberio, now with his own name of D. Juan Pablo Forner — has continued these literary wars in which malediction has won over decorum, and for a time has enslaved reason. . . . Señor Iriarte vindicated himself with *For Just Such Cases Do They Have Trained Teachers*, . . . showing the bad faith of the author [of *The Erudite Ass* and] impugning his various errors and improprieties concerning the use of criticism and the study of the humanities.[11]

Thus, Sempere accuses the author of *The Erudite Ass* of having sinned against everything that Forner holds dear: decorum, propriety, reason, criticism, the humanities. But what angered Forner most was the contrast between the forty-six page article on Trigueros and the meager eleven pages devoted to Forner in volume three of the *Library*. The article on Forner is rather positive in its attitude. There is a somewhat neutral statement about the *Apologetic Oration;* quotations from the *Satire Against the Vices Introduced Into Castilian Poetry*; a resumé of the polemic with Huerta and the *Reflections of Tomé Cecial* that tends to be favorable toward Forner; and a discussion of the *Philosophical Discourses* with quotations. At the end of the volume there is an addendum which clarifies the contents of the appendix to the *Apologetic Oration*.[12]

There is also an article in volume three on Huerta, in which Sempere says that "in spite of its defects, [*Raquel*] passes for the best, or perhaps the nation's least poor work of this kind."[13] Then, without naming Forner or the *Letter to Ayala*, Sempere recalls Forner's critique of the assassin scene, pointing out that Forner was wrong. He reviews Huerta's *Spanish Theater*, taking the point of view that Huerta is a bad collector of plays, and then talks again about the Tomé Cecial attack and the other pieces written against Huerta's work. He suggests that these impugners have missed the point and "wasted time uselessly in accessory things."[14] Sempere offers his own formula for useful criticism, which consists of being much more specific about things like talent, ingenuity, and art, points that "if treated with judgment, opportune erudition, and a good style, would be much more important and much more useful than the vague criticisms and frivolous satires with which the public has entertained itself until now."[15]

III *Forner's Answer to the Trigueros Article*

Thus, the third volume of the *Library* is filled with inconsistencies, while the comments about Forner in the articles on Trigueros and Iriarte in volume six are inconsistent with Sempere's evaluation of Forner in volume three. When Forner answered Sempere in his *Suplemento al artículo "Trigueros" comprehendido en el tomo 6° del "Ensayo de una biblioteca de los mejores escritores del reynado de Carlos III"* (Supplement to the Article "Trigueros" Contained in Volume 6 of the "Essay on a Library of the Best Writers of the Reign of Charles III"), he pointed out these disparities and noted that "great men often think the reverse of everyone, [but] Doctor Guarinos, to be greater than everyone else, has decided to think not only the reverse of how people generally think, but the reverse of himself."[16] He also suggests that it was Trigueros himself who wrote this panegyric in the "anti-Fornerian *Library*,"[17] because Sempere, in spite of his defects, is not "a-divine."[18] There was never any proof that Trigueros did indeed write the article, but on another occasion he had engaged in that frequent eighteenth-century pole-mical deceit of self-praise under a pseudonym. After *The Majas* was criticized in the press, Trigueros wrote an anonymous letter to the *Correo de Madrid* attacking his own poem. He then wrote another letter answering the first, defending *The Majas* as "worthy of esteem."[19]

The *Supplement* is a long tirade against Trigueros and Sempere and the only comments that even faintly resemble literary criticism are statements such as Forner's suggestion that "to utter the words *The Flood, The Artisans, Voyage to Heaven* is the same as letting loose a blast of buckshot against the Muses."[20] Forner also reprints the letter of apology from Florian which points out Trigueros' dis-honesty in using private correspondence without permission.

Although the *Supplement* is made up almost entirely of these per-sonal insults, Forner does offer some observations on the purpose of his criticism. He claims that his censures are always for the purpose of preserving good taste in his nation's literature, and never for per-sonal reasons. Forner also makes a curious admission of his own lack of poetic ability. "Forner pays little attention to his poetry, and is not capable of placing himself ahead of even the least of the good poets of Spain; but he does not have to go to some Trigueros or Iriarte or Guarinos to find out the value of his verses."[21] He goes on to defend his philosophical writings, calling himself one who has "drunk in part from the bitter chalices almost always tasted by those who have practiced philosophy without priding themselves in being philosophers; and for no other sin than that of calling the bad poets bad poets."[22] All these comments have the effect of making Forner appear to be unjustly maligned for his good intentions, for having tried to refine the literature of his country. In his typical manner, Forner saves the nastiest comment for last: "The beetle only loves the manure, and although there are few men who think of themselves as beetles, this does not mean that their number is not infinite, and perhaps those who least think so of themselves are most so. Then, let Señor Trigueros publish his volume and let D. Antonio Varas do his job."[23]

The dispute between these two writers later continued over a discourse published in *La Espigadera (The Gleaner)*, a journal directed by Forner and his group of friends. In a letter to the newspaper *Diario*, Trigueros claimed that the discourse was a plagiarism of his own work. On February 9, 1791 a reply appeared in the *Diario*, signed "J.P.F.":"If I were the author [of this discourse], I would keep quiet and let it go without pouting and crying, and I certainly would not claim to be its true father for fear that the pedagogue Varetas [Varas] would get wind of it and let loose for a third time. . . . But let us not labor the point: Varas is an inexorably fierce pursuer of *artisanists*."[24] Trigueros responded with another letter, and then Forner wrote directly to Trigueros saying that he was not the author of the *Diario* letter and offering to reveal the name of the imposter who signed the letter with Forner's initials. Trigueros answered with a noble, rather pitiful letter censuring him for his generally despicable behavior over the years.

It is time for you to think more about supporting your contemporaries than exasperating them. No one is more unhappy with my writings than I am. . . . You should [take] advantage of the talent that God has given you [and, by edifying and not destroying] you will achieve the name that I desire for you. Since I am an old man, I am giving you — a young man — this advice, to repay you as a Christian should. . . .[25]

IV *The Sánchez Episode*

Forner got this kind of advice from everyone — Floridablanca, Moratín, Jovellanos, and even from Charles III himself — but this time he took the advice.[26] He did not continue the dispute with Trigueros, probably not because of the scolding that he had received from the "Philosopher Poet" but because he was already involved in a fight with someone else — Tomás Antonio Sánchez. Sánchez, a noted scholar and editor of the epic poem the *Cantar de Mio Cid (Poem of the Cid)*, had published in 1789 a *Carta de Paracuellos, es-*

*crita por D. Fernando Pérez a un sobrino que se hallaba en peligro
de ser autor de un libro (Letter from Paracuellos, Written by Don
Fernando Pérez to a Nephew Who Was in Danger of Becoming the
Author of a Book).* This is presented as a manuscript found in a
Madrid bookstore, with notes added by the "publisher." It is a satire
on various forms of writing and on a number of writers, including
Forner. The letter itself consists of advice written by Fernando Pérez
to Bartolo, his nephew, about how to be an author. It is a compendium of every kind of absurd advice, with references to the works of
contemporary authors, and the notes are a criticism of the advice
with more specific comments on the writers themselves.

One note, for example, suggests that "bad models should not be
used, even if they are found in well-printed and even better-bound
books, written by learned men, and published with *the necessary
authorizations.*"[27] This is a reference to the Huerta dispute, in which
Huerta was criticized for having published a book which bore on the
title page the statement "con las licencias necesarias" ("with the
necessary authorizations"), rather than the customary expression,
"with the necessary authorization." That such an insignificant detail
as the pluralization of the word "licencia" would result in a polemic
indicates the extent of the enmity between the writers who engaged
in these disputes.

In the *Letter from Paracuellos*, the satirical intent of Pérez' advice
is all too obvious: do not check the veracity of your historical facts;
always add the flavoring of a few mistakes to hold the reader's attention; promise one thing in the prologue and do something else in the
book itself. There are veiled references to Forner throughout the
letter. In the space of two pages, Fernando Pérez mentions Zoilo,
necesidad-necedad, and *tuerto,* which surely refer to the Florian
letter in the Trigueros article, Forner's use of the necessity-stupidity
correlation in the *Comparison of the Eclogues,* and the "one-eyed"
story in Huerta's *Lesson in Criticism.* Allusions to the *Antisophistry*
include the admonition never to admit ignorance of physics and to
attribute everything to Newtonian gravitation, and a dialogue in
which a Spaniard says that "all this is to adhere to the Creator who is
the cause of causes, which no philosopher should be ashamed of doing, whether he be Christian or not, whether he be ancient or
modern."[28] Fernando Pérez also advises Bartolo that he should attack his adversaries in an "apologetic style" free of flattery and
civility, "for it is not certain that bravery and valor are appropriate in
duels of honor. And so, let the Massons and those who are not
Massons come by the thousands."[29]

Pérez' sarcastic comments about the apologies are not necessarily directed against Forner's *Apologetic Oration*, but Forner's response indicates that these remarks were the ones that bothered him most. His reply was the *Carta de Bartolo el sobrino de Don Fernando Perez, tercianario de Paracuellos, al editor de la carta de su tío (Letter From Bartolo, the Nephew of Don Fernando Pérez, Victim of Tertian Fever in Paracuellos, to the Editor of the Letter from His Uncle).* This is one of the best examples of Forner's ingenuity in developing satirical material for these polemics. The *Letter from Bartolo* is a reply from Pérez' nephew, indicating that his uncle is senile and somewhat crazy. Therefore, nothing that he says can be taken seriously, and it has all been said before anyway, and at more appropriate moments.

It is obvious in the *Letter from Bartolo* that Forner read the Paracuellos letter as a defense of the Scholastics, those philosophers that Forner had attacked in the *Apologetic Oration* and in the *Antisophistry.* Bartolo refers to Aristotle as the "little idol" of the "publisher" [Sánchez], and attacks the Scholastics' uncritical acceptance of that philosopher: "A Bachelor of Arts can very well believe and print that Aristotle was a torch, and that all the other philosophers lit their candles at that torch, because no one is prohibited from believing and printing foolishness. But, in the history of philosophy, one can see that this torch was always several centuries behind all the other philosophers, and that when it took the lead, it was only in the role of lighting up a string of blind men."[30]

Forner then responds to the comments about apologists in the *Letter from Paracuellos.* "If [those apologists] had, in spite of their *stupidity,* written weighty tomes of notes for some silly document about the Cid, I would bet that they would have found themselves immortalized in some *Essay on a Library.*"[31] The *Library,* of course, is Sempere's, which includes an article on Tomás Antonio Sánchez in volume five. Forner's comment is curious, though, because the Sánchez article is not excessively adulatory and even includes some veiled criticism of Huerta. But this is typical of Forner's criticism: he attacks an article which insults his enemy Huerta because that article also praises Sánchez, his present adversary. Forner sees himself as standing alone in the defense of his country, and anyone who criticizes his point of view is the enemy.

It is even more surprising that Forner should attack the *Poem of the Cid* — an epic in praise of Spain and a source of national pride in Spanish literature. Again, this is the result of his attitude toward

Sempere, and this attitude is explained in part by the prologue to the fifth volume of the *Library of the Best Writers*. Sempere makes a rather touching defense of himself: "When [in other countries] I have been showered with praise for [the *Library*] and for other works; and in my country it has been applauded by very few, scorned by some, and I have been insulted with the most base pronouncements."[32] Sempere then talks about his detractors, and they of course include Forner, whose derogatory comments about Sempere are scattered throughout his works from 1785 on.

In the same prologue, Sempere praises France for the way she has immortalized her outstanding writers in the libraries, dictionaries, catalogues, and compendia, and he claims that he has done the same thing for Spain. He criticizes those who say that Spain has no need for the literature of foreigners, those who say that Spain has not progressed at all, and those who have produced "injurious satires, infamous libels against the most praiseworthy individuals in literature."[33] Sempere suggests that he would have escaped all this censure if he had "talked about certain individuals, rendering unmeasured, pompous praise of them, like they have rendered of themselves. Or perhaps portraying themselves in figures baptized with extravagant names, or pretending to publish letters from their correspondants, call them, for example, *intelligent artifices that show the extravagances and disproportions for the benefit of the ignorant common people, or the first of our learned men, pursuers of supersition, and apostles of good taste and philosophy in Spain, etc. . . .*"[34]

This description could apply to just about any of Sempere's enemies, but it sounds remarkably like Forner. Other inflammatory comments in the prologue explain the reference to Sempere in the polemical work aimed at Sánchez: "There are few great learned men and writers in Spain, and if I call the individuals contained in [the *Library*] *best*, I have already explained in another place the meaning that I give to this relative word. To which I now add that I am writing in Spain, and if I were writing somewhere else, I would not put many of them either in the class of *good* or of *mediocre*."[35]

Sánchez responded to the *Letter from Bartolo* with his *Defensa de D. Fernando Pérez, autor de la "Carta de Paracuellos," impugnado por el licenciado Paulo Ipnocausto (Defense of Don Fernando Pérez, Author of the "Letter from Paracuellos," Attacked by the Licenciate Paulo Ipnocausto)*. This *Defense* is a direct attack on Forner and *The Erudite Ass*. According to Sánchez, Forner did in his fable just about everything that Paulo Ipnocausto criticized the publisher for doing in the *Letter from Paracuellos*. In fact, Pérez' letter was "like a mirror, in which authors that read it saw themselves, and some saw that they were one-eyed, and others saw that they were bleary-eyed."[36] The *Defense* goes on to claim that this Bartolo "did not content himself with the baskets from above; rather, he tried to make others of more elegant workmanship. And if he tried to achieve the grade of Licenciate in the difficult science of basketweaving, he could present himself for an examination without fearing that they would throw gourds at him, unless it might have something to do with that refrain about *the scalded cat even runs from cold water*."[37] Sánchez' reference to the gourds is a pun in Spanish — *dar calabazas* — which means literally to give out gourds, but has the figurative meaning of flunking academic work. Forner did not reply directly to the *Defense of Don Fernando Pérez*, but the gourd comment turns up later in the prologue to the *Funeral Rite*.

The Licenciate *D. Pablo Ipnocausto*, reader, was a man born of woman on such and such a day of such and such a month of that famous year in which the sun entered winter under the sign of Capricorn and the earth produced a great quantity of mushrooms and gourds. The contemporary histories do not say whether his birth was an effect of that admirable fertility. What is known for sure is that, at the moment that he was born there were also born an infinite number of gourds and mushrooms, in prodigious masses. These extraordinary fruits multiplied, and he made of them his predilect food and devoured them in such quantity that his friends believed that he was not trying to eat them but to make them extinct.[38]

This progress of the gourd comment illustrates a typical trait of Forner's polemical method. Single, isolated comments such as this often gave rise to responses in other works, which then found their way into still other works, and often were expanded to include writers and works other than the ones first satirized. Thus, the polemics spread and became very complicated, with several different writers participating. The *tuerto* comment is an example of the prolific nature of the insults. This epithet first appeared in Huerta's *Lesson in Criticism* — the attack on Samaniego's *Cosme Damián* — in response to Forner's story about Huerta's play included in the insulting letter to López de Ayala. Forner responded with *Tomé Cecial*, who said that Huerta was not one-eyed, but saw things backward. Huerta reminded his readers of the *tuerto* story in *The Spanish Stage Defended*. Sempere reported the polemic, without using the word *tuerto*, in the article on Forner, then again in the Huerta article, and later in the Trigueros article. Forner responded with his *Supplement to the Article "Trigueros,"* insulting Sempere, Trigueros, and even Iriarte, who at that point had nothing to do with Forner's problems. Sánchez then used the *tuerto* epithet in a note to the *Letter from Paracuellos*, which elicited the response from Forner satirizing Sánchez and, once again, Sempere. Then Sanchéz' *Defense* invented the gourd comment that later turned up in the preface to the *Funeral Rite*.

Thus, this one sarcastic epithet was spread out over eight years (1784 - 91) and occasioned various disputes that involved eight different writers — Samaniego, Ayala, Huerta, Trigueros, Sempere, Sánchez, Iriarte, and Forner. And as the Spaniards devoted their energies to finding a remedy for the deplorable state of literature in Spain, the writer who had started it all, the infamous Masson de Morvilliers, was also always present in these disputes. Forner was one of Spain's most active polemists during those years, but that activity ended abruptly in 1791 when he was given another task to perform, a task which took him away from the battleground of Madrid.

CHAPTER 5

The Last Years: Seville and Madrid

I *A Respite in Seville*

O N July 8, 1791 Forner was named public criminal defender of Seville. He moved to that city and in December married María del Carmen Carassa, whom he described as "a good catch."[1] His marriage gave him three children — Antonio Augustín, Fernando María, and Manuel Luis. During the years 1792 - 94 Forner engaged in no polemics, but he led a very active social and public life. He was inducted into the Patriotic Society of Seville, the Academy of Fine Arts, the Academy of Canonical Law, and the Academy of Ecclesiastical History, and was elected director of the Economic Society. His social life revolved around a *tertulia* that included such well-known literary and public figures as Reinoso, Arjona, Lista, and Blanco White. During this time he also became a close friend of Florian and devoted much of his attention to aiding the French immigrants who came to Seville to escape the persecution that followed the 1789 revolution.[2]

In a letter written in 1792 to Francisco P. de Lema, Forner expresses his contentment during this unusual period in his life. The letter reveals both Forner's sense of humor and his stern, self-righteous attitude toward life.

My esteemed Teacher:

In the little less than a year that I have been in Seville, I have made the following progress. I have written a work that I am going to publish; I have been in love for six months; I married in the seventh month, and in the eighth I turned out to be the father of an embryo that is moving firmly along the road to vitality. I do not know if this enters into the rules of philosophy; for, if we pay attention to the grave pronouncements of some Bourbons of antiquity, and of the many prissy ones of our era, a man should neither fall in love nor get married quickly and unexpectedly, since he cannot resist completely the impetus of a passion that woos and seduces him so. Those who preach the relaxation of customs and work toward changing themselves into blockheads can rave on to their heart's content in their attempts to pervert and distort the order of nature, and even of human society. As far as I am concerned, I am firmly persuaded that women were not created to be sterile, nor men to exist without them; that matrimony is the most sacred, useful, and delightful of all contracts celebrated among rational creatures; and that if the corruption of the world has rained its despicable and pestilent contagion even on the purity of the marriage bed, it is fitting to demonstrate true philosophy, through doctrine and through example; that vice has no power in the home of a virtuous man, and that his probity, understanding, and noble circumspection are sufficient to terrify the lot of those that defame the rationality that they unjustly possess. This is the case with me, for I have no qualities other than true philosophy. I had the good fortune to choose an enormously judicious girl. Her good bearing excited the curiosity of a group of freewheeling young people who tried to throw themselves on my home and introduce in it infamy and disorder. With no more threat than my natural aspect — the concise severity of my expressions, the festive allusions of my yet satirical humor, and the decorous indifference of the very lovely girl — the herd of rabble-rousers fled, and today in Seville my house is looked on with the respect that is owed to a sanctuary of conjugal love. I am telling you this so that you may rejoice in your disciple's adventures, so extraordinarily multiplied in so few months, as you can see. I am very content. May God keep you for many years.

Your disciple,
J. P. Forner[3]

Here, there is real insight into the character of Forner. The ideas about society, propriety, and decorum that he propagated and defended in his works seem to have ruled his private life as well. The work that he refers to at the beginning of the letter is probably the *Funeral Rite,* since he published nothing until 1795 and since there are indications that he worked on that defense of purity in the Castilian language from 1788 until at least 1794.

II   *Godoy and the* Funeral Rite

In 1788, Forner refers to the *Funeral Rite* in a letter to Llaguno: "And my poor history project? Is there hope that I will not have to write the funeral rite for the history of Spain, like I have written the rite for the Spanish language? Some day you will see that book, which I think will entertain you."[4] The next reference to this work does not appear until 1794, when the inquisitor returned the manuscript to Godoy, who was at that time the Duke of Alcudia. Godoy then sent the manuscript to the Cardinal Archbishop of Toledo, who returned it on March 2, 1795, with a notation that its publication would be imprudent at that time. The cardinal took issue with Forner's implication that there were no good writers in Spain, and complained that the satire was too severe and all-encompassing. Godoy returned the manuscript to Forner with the following note:

I am returning the enclosed manuscript entitled *Funeral Rite for the Castilian Language*. I had it examined by an impartial person of importance, and I have been given to understand that for now its publication is not appropriate, although the author is assumed to be very worthy of praise and the work worthy of appearing at times less critical than these.[5]

The crisis was, of course, the war with France, which Godoy would soon resolve, thereby earning his title of Prince of the Peace. Forner replied to Godoy's letter, thanking him for his admonition that the times were not right for publishing the *Funeral Rite* and declaring himself "always ready to manifest how truly I love my generous benefactor, and with what efficacy I will work to accredit my unforgetting gratitude."[6] There is a striking contrast between this letter and the comments that Forner directed against others who rejected him. The difference is the position that Godoy held. Forner knew how to conduct himself when dealing with people of importance and power. He kept his word to Godoy, for he later published a poem entitled *La Paz (The Peace)* with a long, adulatory dedication to Godoy. He also dedicated his *Discurso sobre la Historia de España (Discourse On the History of Spain)* to Queen María Luisa, whose lover was none other than Manuel de Godoy.[7] Forner's choice of the name Manuel Luis for his last child was, most likely, one more gesture to Godoy and his brother Luis, whom Forner had known since the time of the *tertulia* in Estala's home.

III *Forner and Vargas:* The Featherless Crow

In 1795, Forner included more references to the *Funeral Rite* in *La corneja sin plumas (The Featherless Crow)*, a work by "Don Paulo Ipnocausto." *The Featherless Crow* has a preface by the "editor," who excuses himself from offering a "semiacademic" eulogy to aid in Ipnocausto's posthumous fame, but adds that "we have in preparation for the press several works by this greatly celebrated man, whose memory will last, no doubt, to the extent that it be to the glory of God. And, in the first work, God willing, a tremendous funeral panegyric will lead the way . . . ."[8] In the "manuscript" published by the "editor," Ipnocausto comments on his own, unpublished work: ". . . And if a work not yet published, guarded in the desk of its author and unknown even in copies, of which there have circulated only fragments among the papers of one and another curious person, if this work is not sufficient to destroy the foundations of the *Solitudes* [of Góngora] . . . , then let it be resolved by those who do not have flat literary noses."[9]

Forner mentions the *Funeral Rite* here because the point of departure is the same in both works. *The Featherless Crow* was an accusation of plagiarism directed against José Vargas y Ponce. In 1793, Vargas published a *Declamación contra los abusos introducidos en el castellano (Declamation Against the Abuses Introduced Into the Castilian Language)*, which he had entered unsuccessfully in an academy competition in 1791. Forner prints in parallel columns passages from the *Declamation* and from the *Orígenes de la lengua castellana (Origins of the Castilian Language)* of Gregorio Mayans y Siscar to show that Vargas copied entire sections without giving due credit, and even copied them so inaccurately that they lose their meaning.

The Featherless Crow is an important work because it deals with the same question treated in the *Funeral Rite* — the corruption of the Castilian language. And Forner even drags up his animosity toward Iriarte, who had been dead for four years.

Of certain great men, the least of their work is the most worthy of esteem. And, from one learned man in Spain, they have collected and presented to the public even what he dreamed about writing and even the little couplets that he produced in celebration of his corporeal necessities. This to show the respect owed to the residues of a renowned writer, for they even immortalized his excrement in the press.[10]

The bitterness is still there, and the attack on Vargas is no less insulting. The final paragraph of *The Featherless Crow* includes a justification for Ipnocausto's censure of the *Declamation*, delivered by the editor": "What benefit could this have to the progress of knowledge? The only important utility offered by this genre of works is the attempt to prevent the trappings of ignorance, so that in the evaluation of talents the fatuous ones will not be confused with the sound ones."[11] So, near the end of his career, Forner is still proclaiming his prime motive, — to be useful to the world by destroying all that is idiotic, dishonest, and ill-intentioned in the literature of his country. Forner sees himself as a kind of guardian of good taste, intelligence, and edifying values in literature. This rests, of course, on his concept of literature as a tool for educating the people. This didactic concept of literature is particularly important in the theater, which Forner considered to be the prime teacher of the common people, or the general public. This led Forner into his last polemic, a dispute concerning the establishment of a theater in Seville.

IV *Forner and the Theater*

In 1795, a theater was opened in Seville after a period of twenty years during which dramatic productions had been prohibited. Forner wrote a "Loa" ("Prologue") for the opening, in which he defended the theater as a didactic device for enlightening the masses. As a result of this defense of the theater, Forner found himself engaged in a polemic with a group of clerics from Seville, a dispute that produced many pamphlets written by Forner and by his detractors.[12] Forner was also accused of heresy, and in his defense he published a long discourse entitled *Preservativo contra el ateísmo* (*Preservative Against Atheism*). This is an attack on false philosophers, those who have destroyed the "true philosophy" which insures man's happiness. That true philosophy is, of course, just what Forner said it was in his earlier works, the *Apologetic Oration* and the *Antisophistry*: affirmation of the traditional doctrines of the church.

Meanwhile, Forner's play *La escuela de la amistad, o el filósofo enamorado* (*School for Friendship, or The Enamored Philosopher*) opened in Madrid with some success. This play had been written some six years before, about 1790.[13] That was also the year in which Forner became involved in a minor polemic over *El viejo y la niña* (*The Old Man and the Maiden*), a play by his friend Moratín. Moratín had tried for four years to get this play produced and finally succeeded in 1790 with the aid of Godoy. On June 13, the *Correo* printed a negative critique of the play written under the pseudonymn Fulgencio de Soto. Moratín answered the criticism with a long defense of his play in the *Correo* and Forner also defended *The Old Man and the Maiden* in a letter to the same newspaper, using the name Lorenzo Garrote. Forner begins the letter in a familiar way: "I have read with lots of laughs that pedantic letter [from Soto] that you inserted in number 371 . . . and I say that I read it laughing because there is nothing funnier in this world than to hear stupid things spoken in seriousness, or to see someone making magistral judgments and revealing at the same time that he does not understand one word of the material on which he is making pronouncements."[14] Forner then accuses Soto of being one of the poetasters who write plays that fail and then criticize plays like Moratín's out of envy.

The letter from Garrote contains nothing new in the way of Fornerian literary criticism, but it does include some of Forner's ideas on the state of theater in Spain. Six years later Forner would defend the theater as a device for refining the human race, and this letter clarifies his attitude about what kind of theater is capable of doing that. Forner is talking about contemporary theatrical fare:

> You will see things that are not found in Plautus or Terence, nor even in Aristophanes, nor would they be found in Barrabas if he had written plays. You will see jester kings; barbarous and scandalous magnates; semi-gentlemanly artisans; learned ladies; insensate, brutal, and insolent officials; heroes stuck into clownish outfits; the best known histories adulterated; the theater converted into a staging of puppets without heads or feet; confusion; barbarity; ignorance; impropriety; gibberish; deliriums; and stupendously crazy ideas. All this you will see, and upon seeing it, you will be amazed that these are men who have the nerve to criticize *The Old Man and the Maiden*, attributing to it defects that it does not have and trying to suppress it so that the barbarity of the war-horse plays can triumph with impunity.[15]

This was one of the most frequent attitudes toward the Spanish theater among those who aspired to a neoclassic perfection of drama. The lack of regularity in the plays, the mixing of dramatic character types, and the general confusion on the stage were the vices that Moratín tried to overcome. Forner attempted to do the same in *The Enamored Philosopher*. After the play premiered in Madrid in 1796 to mixed reviews, Forner responded to his critics by comparing his play to those of Moratín: "Except for the plays of Moratín, *The Enamored Philosopher* alone and all by itself has more dramatic beauties than all those engendered by the Spanish stage for the last one hundred years."[16]

Forner was still in Seville when *The Enamored Philosopher* was produced, and his old friend Estala acted as his agent in Madrid. In fact, Estala even took the liberty to rewrite parts of the play before the opening and during the first few performances, eliminating the things that he felt would be detrimental to Forner's literary and political career. Estala wanted to have the play published, and he asked Forner to write a prologue for the printed edition.[17] Forner fulfilled the request with his "Apología del vulgo con relación a la poesía dramática" ("Apology for the Masses in Relation to Dramatic Poetry"). This apology is surely related to his polemic with the clerics in Seville over the usefulness of the theater, for he emphasizes the instructional, edifying value of dramatic poetry for the masses. "The purpose of poetry is *to teach by delighting* . . . [and] *to teach by delighting by means of verisimilar action* is the object of the theater."[18] Of course, this idea is not new in the work of Forner. It appears in the *Comparison of the Eclogues*, his earliest work, and in just about everything else that he wrote. And it is expressed over and over in the *Funeral Rite*, the work that he continued to revise until his death.

V *Apotheosis in Madrid*

In July 1796, Forner was named public defender of the Council of Castilla, and he returned to Madrid. He was soon elected president of the Royal Academy of Law, which also awarded him a prize for his "Plan para formar unas buenas instituciones de derecho español" ("Plan for Forming Good Institutions of Spanish Law"). His polemical activity ended, for his friends advised him that the disputes that had dominated his life were no longer appropriate now that he held a position in the royal court. The last year of Forner's life was devoted to public service. His death came on March 16, 1797, the result of a condition that began with an illness back in 1783. There is no documentation to indicate what the illness was.

On May 23, Forner's close friend Joaquín María Sotelo delivered a eulogy for Forner before the Royal Academy of Law. The eulogy was then sent to Godoy, that Prince of the Peace praised so lavishly by Forner, with a request for permission to publish it. On June 28, Godoy informed the academy that, although he had not had time to read the eulogy, they could proceed with its publication.[19] In the context of the almost universal consensus of the previous fifteen years, Sotelo's extravagant beatification of the deceased writer in the last lines of the eulogy indicates once again how intense were the emotions elicited by the personality of this controversial polemist, Juan Pablo Forner.

And you, virtuous and enlightened gentleman, if the weak voices of men can penetrate the silent dwelling of the dead, and if the votes of the living deserve to be heard by those who inhabit the eternal mansion of immortality, receive this simple homage consecrated to you by our gratitude and grief. Your merit and your talent have made you worthy of the respect and esteem of the public, and we wish to be the first to satisfy this sacred debt. We recognize, and we will never forget, the benefits that we owe to you. The illustrious memory of your virtues will never be erased from our hearts, and whenever we hear your pleasant name pronounced, we will say to ourselves: "This was our Aristides, who merged the integrity of a magistrate with a simplicity, candor, and patriotism; this our Socrates, who refuted the audacious Sophists and became the target of their rancor and calumny; and this our Anacarsis, who for having enlightened his country suffered more than once the persecution of the ignorant."[20]

CHAPTER 6

Forner as Satirist

I Forner and His Contemporaries

A S is evident in the previous chapters, the life of Juan Pablo Forner was dominated by a series of polemics. From these disputes came a literature that was very topical and limited to immediate concerns. It is interesting that this kind of literary art — the work written "for the occasion" — is precisely what Forner often attacked. His *Letter From Antonio Varas* censured Trigueros for writing an epic poem about the flood along the Guadalquivir, questioning whether it was in good taste to capitalize on the misfortune of those affected by the tragedy. Forner makes a similar criticism in the *Carta del tonto de la duquesa de Alba a un amigo suyo de América (Letter From the Duchess of Alba's Jester to a Friend in America)* as he satirizes the writers who had written poems about three events that occurred in 1783 — the birth of the royal twins, the peace treaty between England and Spain, and the bombardment of Algiers by General Antonio Barceló: "To what extremes the poetasters have been driven by their execrable hunger for money at the expense of the august babes and of this peace, which has occasioned an even crueler war on good taste and knowledge! Poor Barceló! Who would have thought that the poetasters would get you before the Algerians could!"[1]

Forner could be accused of doing the thing that he censures — writing literature for the occasion at the expense of his victims — but Forner's writings were quite different from those other "circumstantial" works. Trigueros and the other poets purported to be writing serious, heroic poems about the events, while Forner's works were satirical, mock-serious writings designed to denigrate and destroy. Still, they were very limited in scope and intent, almost always the result of some vehement personal feud with one of his contemporaries.

71

Although these disputes consumed much of his energy and left
him little time for more serious literary pursuits, they did have their
reward. They put him in contact with every literary figure of any importance in the last two decades of the eighteenth century. Thus, a
history of his life is also a history of the literary activity of those years
which one observer has called "the Golden Age of the literary
bagatelle."[2] Forner managed to involve himself either as enemy or
as friend with an amazing number of significant writers: Meléndez
Valdés, Iriarte, Iglesias de la Casa, Huerta, Samaniego, Jovellanos,
Trigueros, Sempere, Moratín, López de Ayala, Sánchez, Vargas y
Ponce. It is an indication of Forner's pervasive presence in the
literary milieu of Madrid that not a single important name is missing
from the list of his defenders and adversaries. He was a man who
demanded strong reactions from everyone. Either they were extremely loyal to him or they hated him intensely.

II   *The* Funeral Rite for the Castilian Language

The only work by Forner that can be included in the significant
literary productions of the eighteenth century is the one that he
wrote and rewrote over a period of many years, the *Funeral Rite for
the Castilian Language.* It is a resumé of nearly everything that
Forner wrote, a satirical summary of the points of view with which
he disagreed, and a compendium of almost all the critical attitudes
expressed in his other works; and it has the important characteristic
of being less immediate in its intent. Unlike the other satirical attacks on particular authors and works, the *Funeral Rite* is a more
general commentary of literary trends.

The *Funeral Rite* is narrated by Aminta, who decides to make a
pilgrimage to Parnassus — the mountain of the gods — in search of
Apollo, the Greek god of poetry. Aminta searches for someone to
recommend him, but fails to find anyone on good terms with Apollo
because "in Spain today there is no one who can boast of deserving
the friendship of that God."[3] Arcadio tries to dissuade Aminta, offering the cynical observation that writing useful, delightful poetry is a
thankless job, for if you write well you will not be rewarded, and if
you write poorly you will not be read. Cervantes arrives with an in-
vitation from Apollo to come to Parnassus for the funeral of Apollo's
"beloved child," the Castilian language.

Aminta, Arcadio, and Cervantes begin their journey to Parnassus
and encounter a series of scenes that present object lessons on the
nature of literary art. They see a lake filled with writers who have

been turned into frogs by Apollo as a punishment for what they did in life. The frogs include the writers who criticized works that they themselves were incapable of writing; those who propagated a superficial knowledge in their country; those who corrupted the Castilian language by translating French books; the lawyers who defiled legal language with barbaric Latin commentaries to the point that the common people could not understand the laws; various pedantic humanists and philosophers; and the writers who produced the transient monuments of literature — dictionaries, discourses, miscellanea, and collections of thoughts. As they near the temple of Apollo, they encounter a group of academicians condemned for their vainglory and ambition, but still boasting of their titles and degrees.

In the temple, they find a group of weeping journalists. Gregorio Mayans y Siscar appears and defends the elegance of expression that characterized the Castilian language during the sixteenth and seventeenth centuries. Cervantes takes this opportunity to outline the polemic between Mayans and the *Diario de los literatos (Journal of Literary Men)* concerning Mayans' *Origins of the Castilian Language.* Then they see the group of men condemned to oversee the burning of the body of the Castilian language as punishment for having put her to death. Cervantes gives a detailed account of the way in which these writers managed to kill her.

As they leave the temple they encounter the poet Esteban Manuel de Villegas, who presents a discourse on the historical development of Castilian. As Villegas ends his speech, a critic escapes from his cage and begins to pelt the group with copies of the books and journals that attacked Forner in the course of the polemics. There is a long discussion about the books as they are thrown on a huge pile that will serve as the funeral pyre. A count arrives and reports that the Phoenician and Basque languages are fighting over which will be used in the funeral service. Then the dramatist José de Cañizares appears and reads a manuscript entitled "Reflexiones sobre el teatro en España" ("Reflections Concerning the Theater in Spain"). After Cañizares ends his presentation, one of the spectators identifies himself as Benito Jerónimo Feijoo and participates in a discussion of his faults and failures. This is followed by the appearance of a magistrate burning legal treatises because the lawyers who wrote them studied only law and lacked the necessary broad knowledge of everything.

Apollo ascends his throne in the library and delivers a speech about good taste, forbidding that anyone talk about anything that does not "combine the qualities of goodness, truth, and beauty."[4] Then the funeral procession begins, with a multitude of writers passing in front of the throne in descending order of importance. First come the theologians and the mystics, accompanied by a group of savages from the New World who praise the Castilian language for having brought them out of ignorance and pagan violence; and by Bernal Díaz del Castillo, who delivers an apology for Spain's participation in the conquest of America. Next, the poets: doctrinal, dramatic, bucolic, epic, historical, didactic, epigrammatic; followed by the poetic theorists and then the *culteranos*, who come to be punished for their sins. And finally, the prose writers: sacred orators, ascetics, declamatory prosists, historians, chroniclers, novelists.

The body of the Castilian language is borne in by the pallbearers, Alfonso X, Alfonso XI, Carlos de Viana, and Don Juan Manuel. As they reach the catafalque, the body shows signs of life. Everyone begins to rejoice, and Apollo explains that he afflicted her with a paralysis resembling death as an object lesson to all. They have another chance to save her from death. Apollo then gives Aminta a manuscript to read in place of the expected eulogy for the deceased. The manuscript is Aminta's own "Satire Against the Crude Literature of Our Times." The "Satire" summarizes the points discussed throughout the *Funeral Rite* and includes references to almost all the polemics in which Forner was involved throughout his career.

When Aminta reaches the last line of the "Satire," Apollo starts turning all the offenders into frogs. Aminta feels his body shaking and fears that he too will be turned into a frog, then realizes that it is Arcadio trying to wake him. He finds that he has dreamed the entire episode and makes a vow to write it down just as he has imagined it.

III   *The Influence of Cervantes*

The form of the *Funeral Rite* is typical of a particular kind of literature very common in the eighteenth century in Spain and in other countries. It is a hybrid genre, a sort of "novelistic essay" or "essayistic novel," combining the structural and narrative characteristics of the novel and the expository traits of the essay. Other examples of this kind of literature in Forner's century are the *Historia del famoso predicador Fray Gerundio de Campazas* (*History of the Famous Preacher Fray Gerundio de Campazas*) of José Francisco de Isla, and the *Cartas marruecas (Moroccan Letters)* of José Cadalso. An earlier example of this kind of novelistic essay is

Cervantes' *Don Quixote*, according to the eighteenth-century perspective on that masterpiece of seventeenth-century literature. As is evident in Forner's polemic with Huerta concerning the criticisms of Cervantes in the *Spanish Theater* and the *Lesson in Criticism*, the eighteenth-century critics viewed the *Quixote* primarily as social and literary criticism. Since they believed that Cervantes was, first of all, trying to destroy the pernicious influence of the novels of chivalry, they paid more attention to the critical, essayistic characteristics of the *Quixote* than to the fictional qualities of the world that Cervantes created.

Sempere's *Library of the Best Writers of the Reign of Charles III* contains evidence of this point of view. In the article on Isla, Sempere quotes another critic, the Marqués de Caraccioli, in the discussion of *Fray Gerundio de Campazas:* "This work brings to the reader's attention, in the most delicate manner, all the stupidities and gigantic ideas of certain Spanish preachers. The author, a man of much talent, has composed it to discredit bad sermons, just as Miguel Cervantes wrote his *Don Quixote* to discredit the adventures of chivalry that reigned at that time."[5] In the article on Cadalso, Sempere does not discuss the *Moroccan Letters*, for they had not been published at the time that the *Library* appeared. He does quote from Cadalso's *Suplemento al papel intitulado: Los eruditos a la violeta (Supplement to the Paper Entitled: The Superficial Erudites)*, which is a continuation of a work that Cadalso published in 1772 and a response to Montesquieu's *Lettres persanes (Persian Letters)*. Cadalso is answering Montesquieu's charge that the Spaniards only have one good book (the *Quixote*) and it is the one that riducules all the rest: "Neither is that book the only good one, nor does it ridicule all the rest. The only ones criticized in it are the books of chivalry and some plays."[6]

Forner's debt to Cervantes is everywhere apparent in the *Funeral Rite*. Although the device of a journey to Parnassus had become something of a commonplace by Forner's time, this particular pilgrimage with Cervantes as the guide is an obvious reference to Cervantes' *Voyage to Parnassus*. And Forner's use of the various characters whose appearance occasions discussions of literature and language is reminiscent of the *Quixote*, in which Don Quixote and Sancho travel around Spain encountering people and events that inspire comments about literature and its relationship to life. In Cervantes' work, there is an amazing multiplicity of devices through which literature is discussed. There are characters who comment on

the nature of literary art, characters who comment on Cervantes'
works, and characters who burn dangerous books. Don Quixote and
Sancho show an awareness of themselves as characters in a novel, a
character from the spurious *Quixote* appears in the "real" *Quixote*,
and that false novel is satirized in the Cave of Montesinos episode.
The narrator presents the novel as a translation from an Arabic
manuscript, and includes within the novel actual examples of
different types of contemporary prose literature. All of these
techniques are present in Forner's *Funeral Rite*.

Although it is clear that Forner modeled his *Funeral Rite* on the
works of Cervantes, he uses these techniques in a different way and
for different ends. The *Quixote's* criticism is directed primarily
toward the novelistic prose of the seventeenth century, but Forner's
interest is poetry and oratorical prose. The *Funeral Rite* bears the
subtitle "Sátira menipea" ("Menippean Satire"), a reference to the
Greek poet Menippus, whose fame rests on his having mixed prose
and poetry in the same work. The *Funeral Rite* also mixes prose and
poetry throughout; and just as the *Quixote* includes examples of the
different kinds of novelesque prose popular in Cervantes' time,
Forner includes examples of contemporary poetry and oratory. Parts
of the narrative are rendered in many different poetic forms and
many of the speeches delivered by the characters are examples of
oratorical compositions. Forner weaves the examples of poetic forms
into the narrative in such a way that there is no distinction between
the content of the poetry and the prose. In a similar way, the
oratorical pieces are incorporated quite naturally into the dialogue.
Cervantes, however, presents his examples of current fiction as
stories read or told intact by the characters of the *Quixote*. In only
two cases does Forner follow Cervantes' model of presenting the ex-
emplary material as "set pieces": when Cañizares reads the
manuscript of the "Reflections Concerning the Theater" and when
Aminta reads the "Satire Against the Crude Literature of our
Times."

In each case the manuscript is a work found by one of th
characters, and in each there is a critical analysis of the manuscript.
Cañizares reads the "Reflections" to show that it is a valuable piece
of dramatic theory, even though it reflects negatively on his own
plays: "I found this paper . . . attached to a small folder of
manuscripts; I read it and my anger toward myself was so great that
I ripped to bits as many of my own plays as I could grab before you
interrupted me. And, so that you will see that I am right, I am

going to read it to you, for . . . its observations deserve careful meditation."[7] After Cañizares reads the "Reflections," Cervantes confirms the ideas presented therein and Cañizares promises to correct his plays so that they will match the perfection demanded by dramatic art.

The author of the "Reflections" is not named in the *Funeral Rite*. This theater manuscript is, in fact, an article that Forner published unsigned in 1790 in his journal, *La Espigadera*. Aminta (Forner) acknowledges that he is the author of the satirical poem. When he is reluctant to read it aloud, Apollo assures him that he approves of "the material and the just indignation in these verses, and this is sufficient for the needs of the present moment."[8] Apollo is so inspired by Aminta's recitation that he begins converting to frogs all the writers who have committed the sins censured in the poem. This is a remarkable bit of self-adulation, for Forner portrays the god of poetry himself demonstrating the efficacy of this satirical poetry.

Like Cervantes, Forner inserts into his fictional world critical evaluations of his own work. However there is a fundamental difference between Cervantes' techniques of self-criticism and those used by Forner in his Menippean satire. To comment on his own work, Cervantes creates fictional characters. Forner has actual historical personages — Cervantes, Villegas, Cañizares — make the commentaries. Even Apollo is not a fictional character invented by Forner, but a personage taken from the Greek mythic tradition. This is the only case in which Forner uses real historical figures to voice his criticisms. His more usual technique is to invent a fictional character to comment on his own work and on the writings of his contemporaries. The *Funeral Rite*, a very complicated piece of satire, uses this technique as well. Aminta and Arcadio are fictional characters created not by Forner, but by Paulo Ipnocausto, who is himself another fictional character, created by the true author, Forner.

There is yet another level to this fiction. The Menippean satire itself is prefaced by two short pieces — an unsigned "Funeral Oration" which calls the satire a monument to the grandeur of the Castilian language, and a "Notice About the Licenciate Paulo Ipnocausto." The author of this notice is a legatee entrusted with the care of Ipnocausto's documents. The notice is a critical essay on the *Funeral Rite*, in which the legatee utters the most absurd criticism imaginable and accuses Ipnocausto of being a complete idiot. To prove his point, he offers examples of the "extravagant, outrageous opinions" contained in Ipnocausto's writings. These opinions are that only those who know the art of perfecting man as an individual and as a member of society should make the laws by which men will be governed; and that without the practice of eloquence and the speculation of poetry, the writings of men of letters will not be distinguishable from the discourses of the vulgar and ignorant.

All this has two ingenious effects. It creates multiple levels in the fictional world, with the legatee evaluating the manuscript of the Menippean satire written by Ipnocausto, and the characters in that satire evaluating other manuscripts; and the satirical *Funeral Rite* becomes the object of another satire, written by this legatee, who has to be either stupid or consummately ignorant. This is Forner's way of confirming the validity of the very opinions that are being satirized. It also tends to be self-protective, since Forner is offering some very silly criticisms of his own work before his enemies have the opportunity to do so.

These devices are not unusual in the work of Forner. He uses the same legatee to present one of his last pamphlets, *The Featherless Crow*, the attack on José Vargas y Ponce's *Declamation Against the Abuses Introduced into Castilian*. The legatee opens his prologue with a statement similar to the first lines of the "Notice" to the *Funeral Rite*: "Among the many and very extraordinary papers of which the Licenciate Paulo Ipnocausto made me the heir, the present one, if not the most important, is at least . . . Stop right there! (the *curious* reader cuts me off here) And with your kind permission, Mr. Editor, what kind of bird was this Licenciate Ipnocausto? Let us first know the name of the artifice, and then we will know if *we are going inside to see the play* . . . In truth, friendly reader, that curiosity is not impertinent; and it is not unreasonable to ask first the identity of the author of a work, because even though I have read in more than a hundred stupid modern papers that the name has nothing to do with the merit of the writing, still, he who knows that he is going to take Cicero or Cervantes in hand, or some other heavy canonized by public opinion, will read with a pleasant disposition, assured that he will not end up with a headache or the flu."[9]

The earliest example of this manuscript device in Forner's work is *The Erudite Ass*, which is published by the fictional Don Pablo Segarra as a fable written by an anonymous author. In the prologue, Segarra explains the origin of the work:

This fable came into my hands a few days ago among various manuscripts which I pulled from the ruins of a book store. . . . The author of the fable that I offer to the public, according to what can be conjectured from some signs contained in other little works of his that I have, wrote around the years thirty-eight or forty of the century in which we live. His name is expressed only with initials, which are D. J. P. F., difficult to interpret in a man of whom it is not certain that he has published anything at all.[10]

This note is followed by praise of the anonymous fabulist, along with a justification for publishing a literary work of an obviously inferior form, the fable. He says that the other works of this author have been praised by men like Metastasio, and that he wants to give the public a chance to judge for themselves his merits as a writer.

These characters, like Segarra, Ipnocausto, Aminta, and the legatee, who serve as serious or ironic spokesmen for Forner, could be interpreted as merely pseudonyms. But I think that they are much more than that. In almost every case in which he uses these names, Forner attempts to create a fictional world very much like the world of novelesque fiction. Forner is never very successful, however, for his fiction is always very closely related to specific events and authors and works from his own very immediate experience. This is the reason that the *Funeral Rite*, in spite of its multiple levels of fiction, is more a novelistic essay than an essayistic novel. It is so clearly identified with the real world that it remains a satirical commentary rather than a fictional creation.

Forner was by no means alone in using these fictional devices in satirical criticism. In fact, many of the writers who attacked Forner and his writings used the same techniques. The most notable example is Tomás Antonio Sánchez' *Letter from Paracuellos*. Sánchez creates three fictitious characters in this pamphlet — the nephew, the uncle who writes the letter, and the editor who adds the notes and makes the following comments in the preface: "This year of '89, . . . as I was walking one afternoon from bookstore to bookstore like a little bird from branch to branch, and from book to book like a little bee from flower to flower, I ran across a manuscript bound in parchment, so dirty and poor in appearance as to make one want to throw it away rather than read it."[11] The editor points out that the manuscript letter was filled with errors, such as writing *lengua castellana* (Castilian language) as *yegua castellana* (Castilian mare), and that it is surely ironic in intent, since every piece of advice that Pérez gives to his nephew is just the opposite of the advice that he should give him. "One thing that I want to say — and I must — is that the style corresponds to the material, didactic and familiar. The language is pure, virgin and Castilian. And, in the same way, beware, for it degrades many *petimetres* and *pisaverdes* [men who imitate French customs] who only read French books, or Castilian books *fashioned after the French.*"[12]

The editor is correct in his evaluation. The *Letter from Paracuellos* does all these things, and it also includes some subtle references to Forner, who responded with one of the cleverest satirical onslaughts of his career — his *Letter from Bartolo* — using as his "publisher" Paulo Ipnocausto. Forner takes everything in the Paracuellos letter and turns it around to make Sánchez look extremely silly. Bartolo, the nephew of Fernando Pérez, says that his uncle is just a senile old man who has no training in philosophy or science and spends his time making daisy chains in a sanatorium. Ipnocausto, as the publisher, employs all the devices used by the editor of the *Letter from Paracuellos* — quotations from Latin, notes, commentaries — to parody Sánchez' work. This is a rather amusing case of Forner's stealing Sánchez' fictional characters — Bartolo and Fernando Pérez — and using them against him.

IV   *Calumny, Self-Knowledge, and Social Stability*

Sánchez replied by creating another character, a friend of Pérez, who read the letter from Bartolo and wrote a *Defense of D. Fernando Pérez*. The *Defense* consists primarily of clarifications of the vague references to Forner in the *Letter from Paracuellos*, which included a comment to the effect that some writers — even if they are one-eyed — would see themselves in the letter as if in a mirror. The friend also renders a harsh satire on *The Erudite Ass* in response to Paulo's comment that the prologue to the *Letter from Paracuellos* was too long: "It is pretty hard to be a man thin of memory. Did this erudite and salty poet and profound philosopher not remember that to a work of ten and one-half pages — that is, to a very *scant* work — he had put a very *lengthy* preface of twelve and one-half pages? Well, that is just what he did in that famous libel called *The Erudite Ass*. To this — the libel compared with its preface — we could apply that business about *there once was a man attached to a nose.*"[13]

Sánchez' observation is entirely accurate. Forner had done precisely the thing that he attacked his adversary for doing. This is true throughout Forner's career. He consistently censured everyone else for things of which he also was guilty. The *Letter from Bartolo* is an example of this contradiction. Amid this world of fictional characters created solely for the purpose of attacking other writers, Forner has the audacity to put these words into Bartolo's mouth:

> Anonymous impugners are for the most part a bunch of Henry the Fourths; vile people who look for a disguise in order to avoid discrediting themselves with the infamy of their intent. He who walks with upright intent and plays fair does not need to put on a mask, nor look for disguises of such ilk that they disfigure him completely. And particularly when he is not trying to ridicule a fatuous person, or fight with someone with whom it would be improper to battle. . . . He who hangs his name or the signs of his person at the door of his writings declares himself to be the master of what he says, and if he loves his honor even just a little, he will refrain from attacking anyone with lowly things, with calumnies, with pronouncements, with shameful things, or with irrational eruptions.[14]

Perhaps this astounding passage can be attributed to an ironic attitude; perhaps Forner realized how contradictory and self-incriminating it is. However, I do not think that it is meant to be ironic; but rather, that it is a serious expression of Forner's concept of appropriate satire. The escape valve that he provides is the comment about fatuous people and inappropriate battles. Forner was, I think, convinced that he was justified in using these disguises because of the vile adversaries that assailed him. Or perhaps he believed that his Ipnocausto was no disguise at all, since it was common knowledge that this fictional character was really Forner.

A curious variation on the use of fictional impugners occurs in the *Reflections of Tomé Cecial*, another of Forner's truly ingenious satirical works. This pamphlet is presented as published by Forner himself, and in the prologue Tomé pays Forner a visit. This former squire to Sansón Carrasco, a character in *Don Quixote*, is an aspiring writer who believes that "to be a writer, all you have to do is write"[15] and brings along a bag full of manuscripts. They have titles like "An Effective Remedy to Facilitate the Arduous Operation of Extracting the Hot Air from the Heads of Liter-asters: Dedicated to Those who Think Themselves to be Better Than They Are." Tomé tells Forner that Sansón Carrasco wanted to defend Cervantes from Huerta's *Lesson in Criticism* attack, but that Cervantes did not want Carrasco to dirty his hands, so Tomé inherited the unpleasant task of dealing with a man like Huerta. Then Forner admits that Tomé Cecial is just an imaginary character, and that the true author of the *Reflections* is Don Juan Pablo Forner, "a young man, nearsighted, with sunken eyes, a grim face, thin and tall, with a disagreeable brow, . . . and very much the servant at all times of Señor Huerta, though not at all a fan of what he writes, either in prose or in verse."[16]

It is really a surprise to see Forner strip away the disguise of his fictional character, for this is the only time that it happens in all his work. The explanation probably lies in the importance of what Forner had to say in the *Reflections of Tomé Cecial.* Huerta had defamed Cervantes and questioned the value of a great part of Spanish dramatic literature. Forner considered the theater to be the most *useful* vehicle for educating the masses. He considered Huerta's attack on the Spanish theater dangerous because it could undermine the influence of that valuable tool for instructing the common people while entertaining them. Also, Forner thought that Cervantes, in his comments on the theater in the *Quixote*, was trying to reform the theater for similar reasons, and in spite of this, "his zeal — which should have been rewarded with a statue — instead is rewarded with the *Lesson in Criticism*, a cruel invective against his memory. . . . But, long live the zeal of the immortal author of the *Quixote*, and would to God that he had been as successful in putting an end to those comic deliriums as he was in anihilating the inept mob of chivalric writers!"[17]

Forner also censures Huerta's criticism of Cervantes on the grounds that the Spaniards should not detract from the worth of the only writer who is well known and respected outside of Spain. The fame of Spanish literature rests entirely on the *Quixote*, and "the two volumes of itsy-bitsy verses which bear on their cover the portrait of Don Vicente García de la Huerta are not sufficient to replace the two volumes of the *Quixote*. The insipid *Bereberes*, the harlot *Raquel*, the deafening *Endymion*, and the *Balladitties to Lisi* are not among the things that can restore the glory that we will lose if we lose Don Quixote and Sancho."[18]

Forner's concept of the *Quixote* as literary criticism is evident again in the *Reflections*, but there are also some other concepts here of real interest. Forner is suggesting that his satire is directed toward a writer who is doing dangerous things. Huerta has endangered the genre that is most useful, the theater, and he has also questioned the value of the only Spanish writer admired outside of Spain. This clarifies to a great extent the reasons for Forner's satirical invective against Huerta and against almost everyone else. He is attempting to preserve the utility of his country's literature where it is useful, and to purge it of those things that are useless. Later, in his *Letter from*

Bartolo (quoted above), Forner will suggest that the use of vile calumnies may be justified when directed against frivolous writers. Obviously, all of Forner's detractors were frivolous, for his writings are filled with the lowly and shameful things that he censures through Bartolo's pronouncement. In spite of this, he frequently expresses his idea that these things are destructive to the well-being of man as a member of society.

> Human curiosity is of such a lineage of malignity that if it does not believe the calumnies, it does conserve the memory of the accusations, and the victim either loses esteem or is looked on and treated with distrust. . . . All in all, [calumny] destroys the bond of human society, making men look at each other with suspicion, with reserve, with lack of confidence, with caution, and perhaps with rancor and hatred, with ire and vindictive enmity.[19]

This statement in the *Supplement to the Article "Trigueros"* is indeed noble and eloquent, if we forget for a moment who wrote it. Actually, the statement becomes rather absurd, because in the same pamphlet Forner tells a really nasty story about Sempere which seems to be a perfect example of the vice that he censures in the passage quoted above. Forner says that one of his friends bought some pastries and found that they were wrapped in the manuscript of a "Letter to the *Universal Apologist* Concerning its Client DJPF." The friend and Forner go back to the bakery and find the entire manuscript of Sempere's *Library of the Best Writers*, which the employees are using for wrapping their wares. Forner assures his readers that this "fable" is not one of his whimsical inventions: "It is an absolutely true fact, which happened exactly — not more or less — as it is told. The documentary evidence exists in Forner's possession, and he is saving it to show to whoever wants to see it."[20]

Of course, this story about the pastries is so silly that it must be another of Forner's fictions. The technique of ridiculing his enemy's work by suggesting that it is more suited for something like wrapping doughnuts than for reading is very common in Forner's satire. Even more common, however, is the technique of attacking the worth not of the writings but of the writer himself. There is a good example of this in the same *Supplement*. Forner responds to Trigueros' comment about the bad doctrine and worse verses found in the *Philosophical Discourses* by saying that "it should be sufficient to point out that the one who said this is a man who makes *poems about majas* while carrying the weight of nearly sixty Christmases on his head."[21] Obviously, this is not a comment about

Trigueros' poetry so much as an inquiry about the taste and judgment of a man who would engage in such foolish activities at such an
advanced age.

Forner's critical observations almost always end up being very
personalized, and frequently have very little to do with the literature
itself. It seems to be a natural tendency in Forner's work, and in the
work of his contemporaries, to assume that a defective artistic creation necessarily indicates that the artist is stupid. Thus, the satirical
attacks are usually attempts to show how ridiculous the writers are.
The extreme example of this tendency is Forner's most acerbic attack, *The Grammarians*.

V *The Redemption of Iriarte*

The Grammarians was Forner's response to Iriarte's *For Just Such
Cases Do They Have Trained Teachers*, in which the fictional
Eleuterio Geta defended the *Literary Fables* against the attack of
The Erudite Ass. Forner is smarting over Iriarte's criticism of his use
of language, and invents a detailed fictional world filled with
counterparts of the entire Iriarte family, all of whom are more concerned about correct grammar than poetic expression. This fictional
world is particularly interesting because it makes use of the
eighteenth-century motif of the exotic Orient. In *The Grammarians*,
Madrid becomes Peking, France becomes Japan, and the characters
include Kin-Taiso — the mouthpiece for Forner, Chao Kong — who
represents Juan de Iriarte, and Chu-Su — Tomás de Iriarte in the
disguise of a young student learning to be a poet. The portrait of
Chu-Su is mercilessly satirical. He listens to a long critique of
Iriarte's much-acclaimed poem *Music*, a critique that points out
every possible error and idiotic trait, and then declares that he will
take on the task of translating this excellent piece of poetry for the
benefit of his countrymen.

Forner does not sustain his satirical fiction very well, for there are
many moments in which the narrator — who is all too obviously
Forner himself — steps in and delivers essayistic asides to criticize
Iriarte's works and defend his own. After a detailed examination of
the *Literary Fables*, Forner addresses Iriarte's fictional correspondent:

Yes, Señor Geta, let them write to their heart's content simplistic truths
about insignificant subjects. But whoever writes them, may he not presume
to be a great man, rather insignificant and simplistic. They may compose

good fables or bad, cold or warm, cooked in snow or in fire, however you want; but he who composes them should not represent himself in the first of them as an elephant intent on instructing the beasts, but rather as a frog who chooses to imitate the ox blowing hot air or the raven crowing, just because he has nothing better to do. This is what I mocked and will always mock — if God does not remedy it — as long as there are pen, ink, and paper in the world, all the days of my life.[22]

Here the emphasis is on the writer, not on what he writes. In a final attempt to make Iriarte look ridiculous, Forner has Chu-Su undergo a conversion experience at the end of *The Grammarians*. A Spaniard arrives in Peking and offers to take Kin-Taiso and Chu-Su on a world tour to aid in his education. They end up in Madrid at the precise moment that *The Erudite Ass* and *For Just Such Cases* appear. Chu-Su reads them, and then the Spaniard gives him a manuscript to read, a "Brief Dialogue Concerning an Epistle Which, Besides Being Pathetic, Admonitory, and Critical, Also Has the Amusing Traits of Being Leaded, Ferrous, Frigid, Quixotic, Thrasonic, and Pyrgopolynicitic."[23] Chu-Su reads the dialogue, which is a critique of *For Just Such Cases* with a point-by-point rebuttal of its attack on *The Erudite Ass*, and then expresses his disenchantment and self-discovery:

"My unbridled pride! Who am I to believe myself to be the only wise man in the nation, I who only know tractlike literary forms, and no methodical and usefully learned science? A new life and a new method of study!"

In effect, he made a firm and grave pledge to observe moderation with everyone, to free himself from the vanity that made him ridiculous, not to mistreat any studious person with denigrating pronouncements, to study more and show off less, to apply himself to the decency of the severe muses, to renounce sonorous bagatelles, to write not from whim but from respect for others, not to proclaim his things scorning those that are not his, to subject his writings to the judgment of truly wise men, not to boast of his authority among ignorant people, to be humble, moderate, docile, judicious, solid, and finally, to study with the sole objective of being useful rather than for the ridiculous purpose of being considered an oracle.[24]

In this catalogue of the things that Chu-Su resolves to do there is the implication that Iriarte does not do any of them. Here Forner has created a character who criticizes his own behavior and confesses his own sins. This becomes a moral lesson for Iriarte, but it could also be a moral lesson for Forner, whose writings reveal the same tendencies censured in *The Grammarians*. But Forner did not see himself as clearly as he saw others, and he always thought that his sole objective was to be "useful" to his nation's literature by destroying those who represented a pernicious influence.

Throughout these campaigns to refine literature, Forner's technique almost always included this creation of fictional characters to whom he could attribute his own wise judgments and the ridiculous attitudes of his victims. In this way he could be useful — by refining and purifying the literary expression of his contemporaries — and entertaining — by delivering his censures through a world peopled by ingenious fictional creations. Throughout Forner's work there are statements which attribute this same critical pose to Cervantes. Forner surely considered himself to be within the Cervantine tradition, and no writer could aspire to a finer role than that.

CHAPTER 7

Forner as Literary Critic

I *Poetic Theory: The* Comparison of the Eclogues

ALMOST everything that Forner wrote deals in some way with literary theory. Although his satire inevitably becomes an attack on the writer rather than the work, it is always based to some extent on his concept of what literature should be. There are a few moments in which he discusses theoretical questions concerning artistic creation, and he often refers to these problems in passing. The greater part of his literary criticism is an evaluation of the way in which his contemporaries do or do not adhere to his own theory of literature. There is also a great deal of criticism of his adversaries as literary critics, of the way that they evaluate the literature of others. Thus, Forner plays three different roles as a critic: he is a literary theorist, a critic of literature, and a critic of literary critics. The way that he plays the last two roles is ultimately determined by the first — his concept of what literature should be.

The three works that deal primarily with literary theory remained unpublished until after Forner's death. These works — the *Comparison of the Eclogues, The Grammarians*, and the *Funeral Rite* — could not have had very much influence during his lifetime, for they had only a very limited circulation in manuscript form. They are important, however, as an expression of certain critical attitudes that clarify many of the concepts that appear in his published works. And, they are representative of a point of view held by a significant number of literary men in Spain during the eighteenth century. Forner did not create that point of view. He inherited it and did everything he could to propagate it and rescue it from the widespread tendencies to ignore it or destroy it.

Toward the end of the *Funeral Rite*, as Aminta and Arcadio watch the procession of writers filing in for the ceremony, Aminta offers a commentary on Spanish eloquence. This is directed in particular to the prose writings, but the ideas expressed here coincide with Forner's concept of literature in general. "In summary, Spanish eloquence consists of *propriety* of words, gravity of sentences, choice of locutions, breadth and harmony of parts, vividness and power of images, *decorum* and facility of narration, *natural quality* of adornments, and finally, of saying only *what should be said* in the way that it should be said."[1]

The italics are mine, but they could well be Forner's, for they summarize his attitude toward literary art and they are the basis of all his activities as the guardian of useful literature. Propriety, decorum, natural quality, and what should be said are expressions of a single idea that was a principal concern of the neoclassic age, the concept of good taste in literature. Forner's "history" of Spanish literature in the *Funeral Rite* is a commentary on the extent to which the writers of his country did or did not achieve that ideal.

Forner is never very clear about the meaning of these terms. He often defines decorum as that which should be said, and then he defines that which should be said as decorum. These words are almost always used in a very subjective way, and the arguments always end up being very circular. Only in the *Comparison of the Eclogues* does Forner deal specifically with these concepts. This response to Iriarte's *Reflections Concerning the Eclogue Entitled "Batilo"* is Forner's first attempt at literary criticism and it is by far his most erudite. The *Comparison* has two purposes: to present an exposition of neoclassic poetic theory and to prove that Iriarte's poem fails to adhere to that theory. Forner frequently falls into sarcastic comments about Iriarte himself, but if we discount those moments the *Comparison* is a model of literary criticism. After a brief introduction, Forner devotes one-third of the work to a presentation of the precepts for the eclogue form, and the remaining two-thirds to an application of those precepts to the two eclogues, Iriarte's and Meléndez'.

Forner's discussion of poetic theory is the most interesting part of this work, for it presents concisely the ideas that will be the foundation of his literary criticism throughout his career. According to Forner, the essence of a poem is its subject matter, its constitution, and its style. The subject matter is dependent on the ingenuity and inspiration of the poet; the constitution (or composition) depends on the rules of art; and the style depends on the joint manifestation of the subject matter and the constitution. In other words, style is a result of the marriage of content and form.

In the *Comparison* Forner deals extensively with the question of verisimilitude, which is "nothing but the imitation of the universal."[2] This means that the poem presents an example which is universally true, a model which is a "happy medium' *(justo medio)* between the extremes of rigorous realism and exaggerated idealism. The universal represented in the poem cannot be a particular case, but an example that has the greatest possible identification with all cases in life itself. In talking about the two eclogues, Forner uses the example of the rustic shepherd. The poet must not reproduce the shepherd as he really is, for that would be offensive in its rusticity. Nor can he present him as elegant and refined, for that would constitute inverisimilitude. The poet must find that happy medium in which the shepherd is refined enough not to offend the reader's sensibility, yet rustic enough to *appear to be* true to life.

In this concept of art, the reality of the poem is a refined and idealized version of the real world that a wide spectrum of educated readers will recognize as a possibility, a model for the real world rather than a faithful copy of reality. Only through this kind of model can poetic art achieve its aim, which is to delight by not offending, and to educate by presenting an ideal that is achievable. This is the concept of art that is the essence of neoclassic literature — the *utile dulci.* All of Forner's theoretical writings and most of his statements concerning the literature and literary criticism of his contemporaries are based on this point of view — that the purpose of art is to entertain while teaching, to teach while entertaining.

This concept of art explains Forner's concept of style as expressed in the *Comparison.* Style is the union of form and content in perfect balance, in a way that teaches and entertains. Perfect style is, in effect, a perfect execution of the *utile dulci.* The content, which results from the artist's ingenuity and talent, teaches and entertains. The form, which results from an adherence to the rules, also teaches and entertains, for it is a model of perfection, a reflection of a perfect world which is by its very nature pleasing and entertaining.

In the *Comparison of the Eclogues,* Forner outlines in great detail the precepts for the eclogue form. Never again does he give such a complete treatment of a particular literary form. Rather, he places all his emphasis on the concept of the *utile dulci* itself. However, in spite of the thoroughness of his discussion in the *Comparison,* Forner is never very clear about this union of form and content, or about precisely what form and content are. In Forner's literary theory here and elsewhere, content seems to be limited to the ideas themselves and form is everything else — the structure of the work, the language, the plot, the characterizations. This is important, because all of Forner's serious statements about literary theory can be reduced to the one cardinal principle that art should be *useful*, and that means that it teaches the right things. This will necessarily be pleasing; the reader will respond with delight to these "right things," for these things are innately delightful. Forner's literary criticism always turns out to be a critique of ideology, hence the emphasis on content rather than form.

II *Inspiration and Decorum*

Forner was not alone in his tendency to place more emphasis on ideology than on form. This was the trend of his century and was the result of the prevailing attitude toward art and its relationship to society. Literature, like all the arts, had an important role — to educate the individual to be the best possible social man — so literature justified its existence primarily through the values that it taught. The great attention given to the precepts of art, however, indicates that the way in which those values were presented was also quite important. This can be somewhat misleading, however. The precepts generally were accepted as a priori pronouncements, and literary criticism with respect to form usually limited itself to an evaluation of whether or not a particular literary work did indeed follow those precepts. The best known book of rules in Spain was Ignacio de Luzán's *Poética (Poetics)*, and the critic had the relatively easy task of simply checking the precepts to see if the work remained faithful to them. Naturally, this resulted in very little creativity in formal literary criticism.

This kind of artistic theory also puts severe limitations on the individual creativity of the artist. The history of eighteenth-century art could perhaps be told in terms of the artist's struggle to meet the challenge of exercising his creativity without exceeding the established limits of the precepts. Forner's history of Spanish literature — the *Funeral Rite* — does precisely this. It tells the story of his nation's literature in terms of how the Spanish writers did or did not preserve good taste by achieving a perfect balance between their inspiration and the decorum of the precepts. At one point Cervantes advises Aminta to "give full reign to the inclination of your talent,

always carrying it along the path of good taste and reason."[3]
Throughout the *Funeral Rite*, Forner's characters express the idea
that ideal art, useful art, is a perfect marriage between talent and a
sense of decorum. This ideal union is the essence of good taste.

At one point, while discussing the *Teatro crítico universal*
(*Universal Theater of Criticism*) of Feijoo, the count delivers a discourse on good taste:

> The rules of art owe their origin not to the arbitrary whim of man, but
> rather to that very universal taste which leads everyone to approve of the
> same things. This [universal taste] — let us call it a *rational instinct* — re-
> quires no other justification for its decisions than that of constant observa-
> tion, for the fundamental elements of the arts are bound to be the same
> among all peoples who cultivate them, [even though] the forms and
> modifications will be different.[4]

This decorum, then, is a "rational instinct," something that is innate in all men, but also survives the close scrutiny of reason, and is
refined through the constant observation of this rational, instinctual
quality at work in all peoples. Once again, we have a kind of circular
argument: good taste is an arbiter of good taste. Decorum maintains
decorum. Good judgment is nurtured through the observation of
good judgment. This rational instinct is a perfect balance of reason
(the precepts) and instinct (inspiration). Reason prevents an unbridled expression of inspiration, and inspiration prevents a cold,
mathematical expression of the rational.

The count also brings up the problem of originality. Mayans discusses this same problem earlier in the *Funeral Rite* when he defends
his *Origins of the Castilian Language*:

> The precepts of the arts are universal, the applications infinite. If to write
> a history, instead of imitating the skill of the application perceived in
> someone else's historical work, I set out to counterpoint the turn, the order,
> or the constitution of his work, what will I be but a slave to the invention of
> another, subject to falling into his defects and oversights?[5]

The writer has an infinite number of possibilities for applying
these rules and developing an artistic work within their confines. If
previous works succeed in the application of those precepts, a writer
should imitate the "skill of the application," not the application
itself. In other words, he should observe the *way* in which other
writers have achieved that balance of inspiration and precepts, and

he should imitate the principle, not the work itself. Arcadio later expresses the same idea: "True imitation consists of trying to acquire the excellence of others with the same means and by the same path that the previous possessors of excellence did. . . . Education must inspire from a young age correct ideas of the arts, in order to understand their use and their application. . . . "[6] Thus, the *utile dulci* does not only give lessons in life, it also gives lessons in how to create lessons. It propagates itself by presenting models for other literary works. The fact that one writer achieves that balance between educating and delighting inspires other writers to achieve the same balance through their own original application of the same principles.

In spite of Forner's insistence on the precepts as boundaries to prevent a tasteless delirium of unbridled inspiration, Arcadio does provide some relief, suggesting that occasional flights of excessive talent can contribute to a work of art:

Genius dictates to the great poets the locutions appropriate to the images that they portray in their verses. Without any particular study, they are able to say what they should say. Then, caught up in the heat of fantasy, they involuntarily produce those vivid expressions with which they startle us. These expressions contain a grammatical fault? Go tell the versifiers that the fault is at that point a beauty, for even if the poetic construction is irregular, sometimes it expresses a vivid image through its very irregularity.[7]

One reason for this concession to irregularity is surely Forner's polemic with Iriarte, in which Forner was criticized for the kind of grammatical fault that Arcadio is talking about.

III   *Regularity and Originality:* The Grammarians

The Grammarians is a good example of Forner's almost neurotic defensiveness about his own work. It is important to examine what Iriarte said in *For Just Such Cases Do They Have Trained Teachers* to see what made Forner so angry. First, Geta [Iriarte] attacks the critical abilities of the "editor" of *The Erudite Ass.* He agrees with Cisneros [Iriarte] that Forner's fable is "a general and bulky critique which presents no individual proofs of what it affirms, nor any scientific and documented examination of the works upon which the censure falls, [and] it does not deserve a reply. For one can respond to absolute propositions and to personalities only with similar things, and this is not the custom among good critics, but only among people of poor breeding and poorer logic."[8] Cisneros has more *useful* things to do than satisfy transient pamphlets that, discrediting themselves, are born today and die tomorrow. *The Erudite Ass* is defective primarily because it is so limited in its application: "The essential difference between your fables and the one which D. Pablo the fabulist throws at you is that you have composed yours in a way that leaves the readers the liberty to apply them according to their conscience to whomever they please. On the contrary, the one who wrote the fable of *The Erudite Ass* went to great lengths to put it in terms that wrest from the public the liberty of making an application other than one that the author wanted."[9] Furthermore, the author has himself generally praised "established principles very opposed to healthy criticism and good taste in literature."[10] The author knows very little about poetics, for he has suggested that there are no precepts for the fable form. "Before having pronounced so absolute a maxim, he should read and reread the masters of poetic art, and he would see if there are rules for writing fables."[11] Geta then talks about his own study of the precepts and refers to Forner as "one who writes without rules and shows a scorn for art."[12]

In effect, Forner is a bad critic, his fable is not useful, he shows signs of bad taste, he praises himself, he knows nothing about the precepts, and he scorns art itself. Iriarte attacks Forner in a very effective way — he accuses him of having sinned against everything that Forner thinks is important. And there is an even more serious charge in *For Just Such Cases*: that Forner's linguistic abilities are deficient. Of the fifty-three pages in Iriarte's work, about ten deal with the use of language, and about four of these are an examination of the language of *The Erudite Ass*. He points out strange words and locutions, and even accuses Forner of using a language filled with Gallicisms. Forner's response was to turn Iriarte and his entire family into a bunch of grammarians more interested in the rules of linguistic expression than in the talent and inspiration exibited by the work of art.

Even though the point of departure of *The Grammarians* is the question of the purity of linguistic expression, Forner also deals with other problems of poetic art. In response to the title of Geta's pamphlet, Forner creates a "trained teacher," a professor of grammar whose dedication to grammatical studies has robbed him of everything else. The teacher is preparing to instruct Chu-Su [Iriarte] in the art of grammar, and Forner's narrator observes that "too much accumulation of little rules and regulations in the memory interferes with talent and does not let it work freely. The preceptists are always hesitant to sin against the rules, and from this comes an extremely frozen coldness that reigns in whatever they write and which they baptize with the name of *exactitude*. They refuse to understand that an inexact rapture of Homer equals all the exactitudes of the most exact poets. . . ."[13] This trained grammarian then tells Chu-Su:

> I have recognized in you a particular talent for poetry . . . and I could teach you the art of reasoning, without which I have heard that neither good syllogisms nor good verses can be composed. But on top of having forgotten that art through the continual application of myself to severe studies of grammar, I hold as frivolous the opinion of those who believe that it is necessary to reason in order to write poems. For what do all those subtle precepts have to do with the fictions and flights of poetry . . . ? What importance is there in a poet's knowing and distinguishing the quality of ideas, combining, deducing, defining, dividing, ordering, avoiding the errors of the senses or the imagination or talent or judgment (errors into which poets do not fall except by some miracle) and all those other impertinent things that do nothing but waste the time better spent on better doctrines. Learn to put one thought after another and you have got it: you possess art without having to bother with learning it.[14]

In this ingenious piece of satire Forner uses grammar as a metaphor for the precepts of art and satirizes the excessive attention to those precepts at the same time that he affirms their value when they are properly applied. Throughout the writings of Forner, this is a constant theme. The precepts have their proper place, but exaggerating their importance results in a frozen poetry lacking in inspiration. The balance is the most important thing. In the *Reflections of Tomé Cecial* Forner says that "we are superior to all nations in invention, vivacity, and wit, but Cervantes wanted these good qualities to be joined with prudent regularity, which was completely abandoned in his time, and he clamored for reform."[15] In the *Funeral Rite*, Mayans attributes the corruption of historical and philosophical writing to the exercise of "talent and ingenuity without any judgment."[16] In the *Comparison of the Eclogues* Forner calls art "nothing more than nature reduced to precepts"[17] and in the *Funeral Rite* he points out the inherent danger of this: "[in the plaza] nature chose to manifest its preference for beautiful disorder over the symmetrical austerity with which art often debilitates it. At one side the frondose trees were interrupted by the facade of a sumptuous edifice, in which good taste and magnificence were in competition. . . . ''[18]

All this, of course, goes back to the *Comparison*, in which good taste is defined as a happy medium. This belief that literature should be characterized by that perfect balance between art and nature, between precepts and inspiration is the foundation of all of Forner's literary criticism.

IV *The Essence of Poetry*

Apart from the *Comparison of the Eclogues* there is very little applied literary criticism in the writings of Forner. This is curious, since Forner's life was devoted to evaluating the works of other writers. But that evaluation was seldom a specific analysis of literature; rather, it was an exposition of his own concepts of what literature should be, along with pronouncements about how his victims had not been guided by those concepts. These concepts almost always had to do with content rather than form. When Forner does deal with the questions of form, he fails to support his criticism with specific examples of what the writer did, or of what he should have done. Geta's evaluation of Forner's critical method was indeed accurate, which helps to explain Forner's unusually bitter reply. Geta had touched a very sensitive area.

When Forner responds to those very accurate observations, he avoids the issue entirely. The grammar teacher's instructions to Chu-Su are very vague about form. Terms like combining, deducing, and ordering say nothing at all if they are not explained and accompanied by specific examples. And when Forner talks about the essence of poetry, he always explains what poetry is not rather than what it is: "to know how to imprison syllables and incarcerate words, either by study or by natural impetus, is not to be a poet."[19] The same idea is presented through the ironic advice that Forner attributes to the grammar teacher: "the art of making verses is the art of combining syllables; and according to this, it is part of grammar without having anything to do with philosophical knowledge."[20] Earlier, Kin-Taiso had told Chu-Su's father to "make your son a philosopher and you will see him become an excellent poet, if he owes to Heaven some natural quality and inclination."[21]

There are similar comments to the effect that poetry consists of more than just rhyming words and counting syllables throughout Forner's work. He never says what more it consists of in terms of form, but he often points out that the poet must also be a philosopher. Forner seems to have a concept of the poet as a kind of filter for the knowledge of the universe. The poet must possess a vast erudition that embraces the whole of human knowledge, which he sorts out and expresses in a "tasteful" way. This sorting out consists of choosing the things that should be said. Thus, poetry is by definition a model of good taste — good taste in the things that are said and good taste in the way that they are said.

Forner's criticism of his contemporaries is always based on these criteria. This is never very clear, however, because his personal animosity is so exaggerated that it distorts the purely literary ideas to such an extent that they are hardly recognizable. His concept of art is much clearer when he applies it to earlier writers in the *Funeral Rite* and in other works, and he frequently uses the earlier poets as examples of what contemporary poets should and should not do.

One of the best examples of this kind of criticism is the discourse, "Causas del mal gusto en la poesía" ("Causes of Bad Taste in Poetry"). Here Forner makes some specific judgments on the poets of Spain and some interesting comments on the relationship between political power and the level of artistic achievement.

Spain has been very fecund in poets. The fortune of these has varied according to the circumstances. . . . When one writes from pure pleasure or from an almost irresistible inclination, his talent becomes unbridled and governed only by the law of its own capacity. . . . If by chance many of these talents are present in the same century, they gain their place in the common esteem. The art that they exercise tends to acquire such strong vices that it is difficult to eliminate them.

This is what has happened in some branches of our poetry, particularly in the epic and the dramatic. Ercilla, who let flow in the midst of combat the impetus of the star that agitated him, knew no poetics other than his inclination to make verses and his desire to perpetuate the wars that he understood. Since his talent was marvelous, his example was more one of good poetry rather than one of judicious poetry. Valbuena is also admirable in his descriptions and in his stylistic excellences, put on paper whenever his fecund fantasy moved him without reins or boundaries or limits, like one who writes to free himself of the impregnation of his immense accumulation of ideas. Lope, who adulterated art for money and maintained that corruption through whim, did in the epic what he did in the drama. He gave free rein to his extraordinary facility, and left us a greater number of good verses than good poems. Pinciano, who knew well the poetics, was not successful in its application. . . . Those nearer to our era, less learned than their predecessors and given entirely to figures of subtle eloquence empty of thoughts —

figures introduced in the middle of the twelfth [*sic*, for seventeenth] century — did nothing but corrupt the essence of good poetry. . . .

There is nothing easier than making art flower when power discerns, honors, and rewards. But this discernment in the hands of power is the child of innumerable circumstances that do not tend to occur with much frequency. A nation that does not take an interest in humane letters will nurture a wise youth barbarian and crude in its wisdom. It will be able to invent with solidity but with extravagance. It will possess great jurists, but they will be uncultured and misguided. Poetry will have eminent talents, but only a small number of perfect poems. Philosophy itself, which is the master of good taste, will fail in its investigations and dogma. If power possesses a knowledge of the best, and a desire to foment it, instantly you will see a new aspect in the treatment of the arts. . . . Only in this way do nations possess the best works of each lineage.[22]

Here Forner evaluates four poets, and his criteria for good poetry are the same — a union of natural inspiration and an ability to apply the precepts as a rational safeguard against the abuse of that inspiration. Ercilla, Valbuena, and Lope were blessed with unusual talent, but their ignorance of or disregard for the precepts led them to create extravagant poetry. Pinciano knew the precepts but lacked the natural inspiration. Even in Forner's criticism of his contemporaries, if we clear away the comments based on his personal feuds, the same criteria are applied. Iriarte, through an excessive application of the rules to a very scanty inspiration, comes up with frozen verses, quite like the grammarian whose study of grammar has destroyed whatever inspiration he may have once enjoyed.

V   *The Function of Criticism*

When Forner talks about the other critics of Spanish literature, he does so in terms of his own concepts of literature and his own ideas about the function of literary criticism. One of the most interesting passages is in the *Funeral Rite*, when Aminta is confronted with the critic who has just escaped from his cage. The critic throws at Aminta all the journals and newspapers that had attacked the *Apologetic Oration* and then tries to bite Aminta, Arcadio, and Cervantes, barking all the while. This extraordinary event occasions a discussion about critics and the proper function of criticism, during which Cervantes observes:

Criticism, like all the arts, has exceeded its limits in the hands of men, who are always inept at maintaining the proper temperament of things. . . . The gentleman-critic should note the defects of others to aid in the total perfection of literature. But where is the one who criticizes with such a generous purpose? The first intent of the critic is always to discredit the work of others, thereby reducing their merit; the second, to make the public understand that he knows more than those whose works deserve universal esteem, for he proves — so he thinks — that they are worth nothing. Mixed in with these motives are even more indecent passions and designs: envy, hatred, and vengeance. And from this come the calumnies, the pronouncements, the infamous malediction, and all the vices produced, abortionlike, by the intemperance and malignity of perverse souls.[23]

Criticism, according to Cervantes, is one of the arts. It logically follows, then, that criticism should abide by that fundamental rule of art — that it should be entertaining and that it should be useful. Cervantes suggests that it is useful because it aids in the perfection of literature. But the envy and pride of men distort that noble end of criticism and the critic simply attempts to prove that he is better than everyone else. These ideas, of course, sound like Forner's concept of the function of satire, and, indeed, they are the same, since Forner made no distinction between satire and literary criticism. In fact, this passage in which Cervantes offers his own ideas about critics is another example of Forner's ingenious satire. The episode is curiously reminiscent of the story that Cervantes himself tells in his prologue to the second part of the *Quixote* to make fun of the author of the false *Quixote*. In Cervantes' story, a madman drops a marble slab on a dog and then hears his owner insist that he should not have done it because it was a "hound." The dog's owner then beats up the madman, who from that point on runs from every dog he sees, calling it a hound.

The more immediate source of the story is Huerta's criticism of Cervantes in the *Lesson in Criticism*. Huerta said that Cervantes criticized the theater of his day only because he was envious of the success of men like Lope de Vega, and even suggests that this envy motivated him to write the *Quixote*. In the *Reflections of Tomé Cecial*, Forner takes this "criticism-envy" correlation and turns it back on Huerta: "My dear Señor Don Vicente, would you not say that your *Lesson in Criticism* is criticism? No doubt it is, since you yourself have entitled it *Criticism*. Therefore, according to your own words, said *Lesson* is the child of *stupidity* and *whim*, and furthermore, it is a *synonym* of *envy*."[24] Here Forner is making great fun of the idea that criticism is synonymous with envy, but then, in the *Funeral Rite*, he quite seriously puts the same idea into Cervantes' words. Forner surely agrees with his fictional Cervantes that criticism should work toward being useful but that the majority of critics act out of envy. It is significant that Aminta is absorbed in listening to Cervantes' discourse when he is hit with the attacks on the *Apologetic Oration*. The implication is obvious: Forner's *Oration* is one of the useful books that has suffered this kind of unjust criticism. The attacks are motivated by envy and pride, written by men who are incapable of writing useful works.

Later in the *Reflections of Tomé Cecial*, Forner offers another interesting idea about the dangers of criticism as he censures Huerta's negative comments about Racine: "How much better it would be not to reproach these careless moments [in Racine], not to censure him for something that is not deserving of censure, for doing that gives the foreigners the opportunity to feel like expurgating our plays and taking from them enough supernumeraries to populate a colony in America. Criticizing foreigners, I think, should be done with reference to things that cannot backfire on us; because, if we spit in the air and the saliva falls back on us, we will be left more dirty than we already are. To say that Racine *affected regularity and Hellenisms to make up for his lack of ingenuity* is to say that no one, observing propriety, can be ingenious. . . ."[25]

Obviously, Forner's last comment is confused. To say that a particular author adheres to the rules in order to compensate for his lack of inspiration is not necessarily to say that everyone who adheres to the rules does so for that reason. This example of twisted logic is characteristic of Forner's literary criticism, for he was much better at being a literary theorist than at practicing applied criticism. The other comment he makes about Huerta's critique of Racine — that foreign authors should be criticized only for sins of which the Spaniards are not guilty — is more consistent with Forner's own critical methods. He censured their ideology, and in that he felt that he was on firm ground; Spain could not be censured for that, since she had always remained true to the orthodox Christian tradition.

This concept of Spain's literary and philosophical tradition, which I will discuss in the next chapter, explains much about Forner's literary criticism and its tendency to slip into satirical invective. Forner was not very good at applied literary criticism because he was not really interested in all those subtle precepts that he talked about so much. His real interest was in the ideology of the literature that he attacked or defended. His comments about inspiration, precepts, linguistic expression, and style were usually just disguises for another attitude, an objection to a particular ideology.

This is one of the reasons that his concepts of literary criticism are always so confused. He lacked the training and the ability for a careful, specific critique of literature as literature, and trying to make up for that, he turned to satire. It was always easier to simply dismiss the work and satirize the writer than to make a careful analysis of the literature.

CHAPTER 8

Forner as Defender of the Faith

I *True Philosophy and the Limits of Knowledge*

THROUGHOUT Forner's work, the statements on good taste, decorum, and propriety apply not only to the way things are said, but also to "what should be said." There are examples of this in many of Forner's evaluations of the work of other writers: the "assassins" in Huerta's *Raquel* should do their work instead of delivering long speeches; Iriarte's characters in the eclogue talk about things unsuitable in that poetic form; certain things said by Forner's critics would be better left unsaid. All of these statements deal with the question of what is appropriate to a particular literary form: the drama, the eclogue, literary criticism. There is another, much more important dimension to this question of "what should be said," the fundamental problem of appropriate ideology.

In his discussions of ideology, Forner is always conservative and even anti-intellectual. Aminta affords only a very transparent disguise for the real Forner when he suggests that "knowledge is a dangerous occupation and a task of doubtful success, for the exposition of which neither the profundity of knowledge nor the abundance of information is sufficient, if good judgment joined with wise rectitude does not aid in the formation of the work."[1] Here it is unclear whether Forner is speaking of *how* something should be expressed or of *what* should be expressed. Probably both, but later in the *Funeral Rite* Arcadio delivers a long discourse which clarifies this concept of the propriety of certain subjects and the absolute impropriety of others.

The classic books of nations — I mean those books that are useful in all ages and incorporate admirable proofs of the vigor, grandeur, and amplitude of the human mind — . . . propagate languages, indoctrinate peoples, and at all times sow and multiply ideas about what is best in literature. And for the construction of this caste of books to be known, propagated, and esteemed in a nation, it is essential that a certain type of instruction be spread among the people. It is essential that the people possess a number of fundamental notions sufficient for them to be able to distinguish between the regular and the monstrous, the natural and the ridiculous, the delightful and the scandalous, the sublime and the pompous, the verisimilar and the completely portentous, the simple and the cold, and other general ideas of this kind, which are something like a catechism of good taste.[2]

Useful books are those that contain certain ideas, and the people must be taught to discern those ideas. Arcadio assures his audience that he is not suggesting that a nation cannot be glorious or admired without that kind of books, for their production depends on many things. Sometimes it happens, sometimes it does not, because "the progress of knowledge is successive, never achieved in one blow, and the seed that gives origin to these progressive steps has always been the fomenting of those arts which delight as they teach, because those arts incarnate the true exercise of good taste."[3]

Arcadio's rather befuddled reasoning — that this knowledge is propagated by useful books and that useful books are propagated by this knowledge — is reminiscent of the idea that good taste begets good taste. The comment about a nation's glory not necessarily resting on this kind of literature is surely a response to Masson, who suggested that Spain was contributing nothing in the way of literature. The *Funeral Rite*, with all its criticism of Forner's contemporaries, confirms Masson's opinions with respect to the eighteenth century, but Forner excuses that by claiming that Spain is great anyway, since she contributes and has always contributed a great deal by saying those things that should be said.

Of course, the important question is what constitutes that which should be said. Forner's concept of the poet as a philosopher answers that question to some extent, if we are careful to accept his definition of philosophy. In the *Funeral Rite*, an unidentified "learned man" says it well:

Philosophy . . . is the science of truth and virtue. And since truth is difficult to find, and virtue difficult to practice, philosophy teaches one to examine and meditate much and to speak little; to do good work before reprehending in others their ill works. Philosophy is the perfection of the understanding. . . . Philosophy is the perfection of the will. . . . Philosophy is modesty, decency, humility, decorum, propriety, profound examination of things, long and scrupulous experience, rectitude of reasoning. . . .[4]

It is remarkable how often these words *decorum* and *propriety* occur in the *Funeral Rite* and how Forner seems to think that they en-
compass and explain everything. But since their meaning depends
entirely on one's own idea of what is proper and decorous, and since
they are never explained in Forner's work, these words in fact say
nothing. There is another passage in the *Funeral Rite* that makes
Forner's point of view a little clearer. Arcadio, seeing in the procession of mourners three of Spain's most revered mystic writers — Luis
de Granada, Luis de León, and Teresa de Jesús — comments on
their literary achievement.

In [the books of these mystics] there is only one system, which is: to love
the creatures of their Maker, and to love each other, in such a way that they
never do each other evil and always do all the good that they can. Put
alongside this saintly simplicity the proud systems of the philosophers, and
you will see that these systems either come to rest on the simplicity of the
precepts [of the mystics] or, if they depart from them, they end up in
shameful wanderings or interminable disputes. For those precepts are the
soul of the moral part of man, and in departing from them, one cannot take a
step without falling over the precipice.[5]

Philosophy, then, is really moral philosophy or, more specifically,
doctrine. This is evident in the procession line, in which the writers
are lined up in the order of their importance. First come the
theological and mystical writers; then the poets, with the doctrinal
poets leading the way; and finally the prosists, led by the sacred
orators and the ascetics, "those that employed the arts of persuasion
to the material of greatest usefulness."[6]

II A *Defense of Dogma: The* Apologetic Oration

Although in the *Funeral Rite* Forner does deal with what should
be said, the fundamental work on this question is the *Apologetic
Oration for Spain and Her Literary Merit.* This apology for Spain's
literature is not that at all; rather, it is a defense of Catholic tradition
and the pervasive influence of the church in the cultural heritage of
Spain. In the entire work on Spain's "literary merit" there are only a
very few comments about the imaginative literature of the country.
Instead, it deals with moral philosophy and the philosophers who
have affirmed the traditional values of the Catholic point of view.
This was surely the primary reason for its rejection by the academy,
which was looking for an apology for the artistic and scientific ad-
vancements of their country. Another reason, no doubt, was the

quality of the expository writing. They were looking for excellence, and it is evident that they did not find it in the *Apologetic Oration*.

Forner's apology is divided into four sections: a prologue, which includes a justification for the work and Forner's version of the circumstances surrounding its publication; Part I, an exposition of Forner's ideas about what constitute "useful contributions" to mankind; Part II, which duplicates Part I to a great extent but is a more theoretical discussion about the nature of man; and notes on the text. The prologue and two parts total about ninety pages in Zamora's edition and the notes fill the remaining ninety pages.

The prologue purports only to provide a justification for the work that follows, but it actually presents in concise form the ideas that Forner will develop more fully first in Part I, then again in Part II, and then again in the notes. The *Oration* is an extraordinary example of exposition, in that almost everything is stated and restated and then stated again. It is a highly disordered piece of writing and it is based on a very limited point of view, with no critical examination of that point of view.

Since Masson suggested that nothing was owed to Spain after all these centuries, Forner begins by considering the criteria that should be used to determine whether a country has contributed anything to the advancement of civilization. Everything depends on what one means by "advancement" and that depends on one's concept of what is valuable for man. Forner's *Oration* then becomes a treatise on what is of value to man and the extent to which Spain has preserved and propagated worthwhile things.

When we try to determine the literary price of a nation, it is necessary to consider what kind of literature pays homage to the understanding and spreads legitimate good in the human lineage. A nation that has cultivated and continues to cultivate this species of knowledge is wise, extremely wise, no doubt. . . . Elegance that wastes itself on frivolous and harmful subjects is of no merit; and, in weighing on the balance of reason the ways of wisdom of different peoples, usefulness should preponderate over elegant and magnificent vanity, even when it appears in a somewhat careless and disordered form. . . . The purpose of my Oration [is] to demonstrate the merit of wisdom in Spain by [showing] the usefulness of the subjects to which the learned Spaniards have consecrated their efforts. Our learned men . . . have devoted themselves in tranquil subordination to a study of truth and, without doing injury to men, they have worked more than once toward that which is useful to man. Surely this deserves some recognition, no matter what the inexorable Masson may say. . . . Hence [this Oration], this laudable exercise in spreading flowers upon the sepulchres of those who, in Spain, made rationality glorious. . . .[7]

This passage is filled with terms which need some explanation or definition — *understanding, usefulness, truth, reason, rationality;* but the *Oration* is a very representative piece of Fornerian writing, and most of these terms will not be explained. Forner's exposition of Spain's achievements is based on an a priori understanding of what these words mean. The only one that he explains in detail is *usefulness,* and his explanation of this term tends to define all the others. Even this explanation is never stated very clearly, but it can be inferred from comments scattered throughout the *Oration.* In response to Masson's observation that in Spain no one thinks,[8] Forner delivers the following declaration:

It is true: we Spaniards do not think about many things. But if you point them out and name them specifically, you will have an example of our solidity and your levity. *No one thinks in Spain,* that is so: No one thinks about tearing down the altars raised to the arbiter of the universe by human necessity, guided by an infallible revelation; no one thinks about disturbing the public peace, combating with indecorous sophisms the beliefs which give men hope and truth to carry them through the miseries of this calamitous life; no one thinks about ripping from the human heart the natural sentiments of virtue, nor about snuffing out the secret accusations that plague the soul of the delinquent; no one thinks about praising the culpable inclinations by which the fragility of our nature is swept away, if left to its own devices.[9]

Just as Forner defined poetry by saying what it is not, he defines Spain's achievement in terms of what she *has not done.* The implication is that France, the country of Masson the maligner, has done all these things. The list is interesting: the sins of the French include tearing down the altars to God, undermining the beliefs that give man hope in the midst of his misery, depriving man of his *natural* sentiment of virtue, and praising the base inclinations of man's *natural* fragility. All this, of course, is directed toward the writings of the eighteenth-century French *philosophes,* who have destroyed the faith that Spain has always tried to preserve.

This passage also reveals Forner's concept of man, and his attitude toward the "rational creature" is the foundation of everything that he says about the usefulness of the achievements of his fellow countrymen. The first eleven pages of Part II are an exposition of this concept of man. In the margin, Forner has put a resumé of the ideas expressed in the text. This concise summary is an excellent presentation of the ideas that guided Forner throughout his literary career.

Man is an entity composed of two substances, each of which constitutes a certain order; and the true constitution of the human being consists of the preservation of these two substances. * The most precise objects of man's rationality are as many as the relationships to which he is subject and the obstacles which oppose the correct constitution of his being. * The true being of man does not consist only of the soul, but of the union between the two substances. * Therefore, the science of man cannot be reduced to the speculations of his understanding alone. * The legitimate science of man should consist of knowing what he owes to his soul and what to his body, or — in other words — of knowing how he is to maintain the correct consitution of his being. * The science of man is reduced to three ends: to his perfection, to his aid, and to his enjoyment. * Religion and moral philosophy are the sciences that perfect him; that is, they are the ones that maintain him in his constitution. * Man is sociable by nature; the preservation of reciprocal roles maintains the order; and the conjoint of these roles is precisely natural law, which also directs itself toward the perfection of man. From the abuse that man has made of his liberty is born the corruption of his state, or constitution. * Man adulterated the ideas of religion. * Man introduced disunion into natural society and thereby tried to destroy himself. * It was necessary, then, to bridle this evil, and from this came the civil states and the positive laws, which are alterable. * The true idea of religion was lost and a sure way of restoring it was necessary. * The primary sciences directed toward the aid of man [are] revealed religion and civil legislation. * The subaltern sciences and arts [are] necessary for the use and application of the others. * The arts that give enjoyment to man [are] the arts of imitation. * The attempts that go beyond these limits are useless and should not constitute the scientific merit of man. * The sciences and arts are already corrupted beyond their first foundation. * The nation that has given its most learned men in those sciences necessary and useful to the human being, or has tried to reduce the sciences to their true limits and ends, is no doubt the nation that has the greatest scientific merit.[10]

It need not be pointed out that Forner's concise outline of his concept of man and the proper role of science is confused. No less confused is the complete text, which consists of an elaboration of these comments. Forner did, however, have very definite ideas about all this, but whenever he tried to express those ideas in expository form, he was unable to do so. Scattered throughout his writings there are statements which, when they are weighed against each other and then considered as a whole, make his ideas perfectly clear. The basic tenets of his "philosophy" are the following:

1. The constitution of man consists of two parts: instinct and reason.

2. Man is endowed with a natural freedom which permits him to maintain his natural state of instinct and reason in perfect balance, or to pervert his natural state by upsetting that balance.

3. Man is by natural instinct sociable, and this sociability creates in him a desire for a relationship with other men.

4. Man is by natural instinct aware of his Creator, and this awareness creates in him a desire for a relationship with God.

5. Man's happiness depends on his preserving his natural state; the right purpose of knowledge is to be useful to man — that is, to help him preserve his natural balance between instinct and reason, his relationship to other men, and his relationship to God.

III   *The Fragility of Man and the Role of Censorship*

The most interesting aspect of Forner's concept of man is his analysis of instinct and reason. When Forner talks about body and soul, as he does in the marginal resumé, he is referring to the body as the instinctive part of man. The soul, curiously, is one with reason and includes all the reflective, critical powers. Faith is both instinctive and rational. Man believes in God because he has an instinctive inclination to do so, and his reason confirms in him the validity of that inclination. This natural tendency, however, is fragile, for an excessive exercise of man's rational powers may lead him to reject his instinctive attraction to his Creator, or this rejection may come from a neglect of reason, in that man may fail, through not exercising his reflective power, to remain aware of his Creator and the benefit of a relationship with Him.

In much the same way man may pervert his sociability. Through a lack of reflection, man may allow self-interest to replace the necessary right relationship with other men within the social order. The safeguards against man's fragility are moral philosophy, which teaches him the value of a right relationship to God and man, and civil law, which insures that man will maintain a right relationship to his fellow man. This leaves something of a gap, for there is nothing to *insure* that man maintain a right relationship with God. The *useful* arts try to do that by presenting lessons that entertain as they teach. They also present pleasing lessons in sociability, and the man who maintains his correct relationship with God will necessarily maintain a correct relationship with his fellow man.

Of course, all this is very idealistic, mainly because of the fragility that is a fundamental tenet of Forner's concept of man. This leads Forner to expound a very paternalistic view of governmental authority and a strict policy of official censorship. In the *Apologetic Oration*, in response to Masson's comments about the Spanish government's infringement on the right to free thought and expression, Forner clearly expresses his attitude toward censorship:

And will our accusers still try to say that the constitution of our government is barbarian because it protects us from the errors that result from the licentious and unbridled liberty of perverting the most authorized establishments and the ideas that the general consensus of all people has approved as true?[11]

We should not blush at confessing that we are prohibited from reading those books that, if they were not prohibited, would not be read anyway by men who want to conserve uncorrupted the purity of their customs. . . . The most perfect legislation is not that which imposes punishment on criminals; rather, it is that which provides the means by which there will be no criminals.[12]

Censorship is beneficial because it protects man from the ideas that would be harmful to him. In a note to this passage, Forner extends this paternalistic function of government even to what men are allowed to think: ". . . if by *liberty of thought* is meant the freedom to teach and publish whatever one pleases, the supreme potentate can take this liberty also, and direct it in the manner that he considers most advantageous so that it does not injure and so that it is useful."[13]

Forner's attitude is based on the idea that men are not able to judge for themselves what is and what is not useful and beneficial. He attributes this, once again, to man's innate weakness, his tendency to pervert that balance between reason and instinct. In particular, man's curiosity is to blame for this tendency toward perversion.

Human curiosity, stimulated by necessity, slowly emerged from the prison of man's crude beginnings. After it succored the anguish of necessity and provided man with the aids that he needed for his comfortable conservation, it moved rapidly toward introducing him into the countries of conjecture. And, distracted in his search for truth, man followed only the shadows and images of truth. There can be no doubt that mortals owed to the penetrating vigor of their understanding the surety, the convenience, the good that came from contemplating things in infinite ways, from looking through innumerable facades, from reasonings. As a result of a multitude of combinations, these things have become lasting, fatal witnesses of the grandeur of man and of his weakness. His very discoveries moved toward achieving the happiness that he was looking for; and he would have been happy if he had known how to stop his steps toward precipitation.[14]

Man is blessed with contradictory tendencies. His curiosity leads him toward refining his being but it also leads him toward perverting that being by going too far, by not recognizing the limits of the knowledge that will preserve his own happiness. The function of an enlightened government is to establish those limits for man.

The *Apologetic Oration* seems to deal much more with ideology than with literature as such. Forner gives the work the title of *Apologetic Oration for Spain and Her Literary Merit*, however, because all this ideology has a direct bearing on the way that Spain has managed to preserve her literary merit. In the context of Forner's view of the function of literature — to teach while it delights — the *Oration* really is about literary art. Literature is primarily a tool for propaganda, a means of disseminating a particular ideology for the benefit of that fragile, rational creature, man. The *Oration* confirms that Forner was among the most determined advocates in eighteenth-century Spain of an interpretation of the *utile dulci* that clearly emphasized the *utile*.

IV *Forner's Self-Defense: Patriotism and Orthodoxy*

There were many attacks on the *Apologetic Oration*, particularly on Forner's discrediting scientific investigation. One of the most pointed rebuttals was Conchudo's *Letter to the Author of the "Apologetic Oration,"* which censured Forner's scorn of Newton and Descartes and even suggested that Forner was one of those "gothic doctors" who still had their feet firmly planted in the Middle Ages. Forner defended himself in his *Antisophistry* by attempting to clarify that part of the *Oration* in which he placed the study of moral philosophy over the study of the natural sciences. In the *Antisophistry* he makes a definitive statement on his concept of what is important in the search for knowledge.

I will make a brief analysis of the ideas [of the *Oration*] in order to clarify this truth. God, man, and nature are the three objects of the philosophy of the human species. A clear and distinct idea of Infinite Being, some irrefutable proofs of the attributes of the Creator, and some exact notions of His providence and influence in our operations are the first knowledge that we should foment, for the omnipotence and goodness of the Supreme Being requires that the dependent creature make this tribute. If to this end we paint the origin of the corruption of human nature, and the ineffable means of its reparation, we must add to that study another one, one even more superior and indispensable for our true happiness. These principles would be useless if man, little inclined to follow his model, abandoning his obligations and failing to conform to the rules that those obligations prescribe for him, should only act through instinct, almost without distinguishing himself from the beasts. He needs to fix himself on certain general principles from which he can deduce many others so that all of them together will form the plan that should serve as a norm for his actions. Being, on the other hand, sociable, and not being able to compose for himself independence and security, he needs a certain superior power to protect him and elevate him above the dangers to which solitude would expose him. This power cannot exercise its influence except by means of certain declarations of his will, which should be understood differently by all those that constitute the social contract. It is, then, inescapable that the study of religion, and of the ethics of man and of the citizen should serve as the basis of our knowledge.[15]

It is significant that Forner presents this passage as an attempt to clarify what he said earlier in the *Oration*. The explanation is vague and filled with dogmatic statements presented without any critical analysis. Forner is simply restating his concept of man's happiness as being derived from a right relationship to God and to society, a relationship that can be achieved only through an affirmation of Catholic doctrine. What this passage does clarify is that Forner's defense of his country is really a defense of his religious convictions. This is, in fact, an appropriate answer to Masson, since the greater part of that encyclopedia article was based on the idea that Spain's ills were all derived in some way from the power of the church and its institutions.

The *Antisophistry* is very important to an understanding of Forner's ideology. If we accept the premise of this work — that revealed truth is supreme — all of Forner's other anti-intellectual, antiscientific attitudes make much more sense. Forner published the *Antisophistry* in 1787, the same year that he finally managed to get into print another work written seven or eight years before, the *Philosophical Discourses Concerning Man*. The *Philosophical*

Discourses are in the form of a long poem with extensive notes in prose in which Forner expresses in much greater detail the ideas found in the *Antisophistry*. These works, together with the *Apologetic Oration*, clearly demonstrate the reason for Forner's objections to Masson and to the entire French Enlightenment: his fear of what the widespread acceptance of science and "new philosophy" would do to revealed truth.

Forner maintained these attitudes throughout his career. In 1795 he was accused of heresy, probably because of his dispute with the churchmen in Seville over the licitude of the theater. To absolve himself of this charge he published a treatise on theology, the *Preservative Against Atheism*. This is a compendium of his ideas on doctrine and the role of government in preserving the purity of belief. The concepts have not changed since the *Apologetic Oration*, but Forner seems to be more interested in politics than before. The "preservative" that Forner proposes is twofold: an acceptance of "true philosophy" and a government that will use its power to insure that acceptance. In the "Preamble" to this work, Forner outlines the first cause of heresy, the fragility of man's nature:

All the peoples and nations that have ever existed on the face of the earth have experienced in different times and in different circumstances the miserable effects of man's weakness and decadence. . . . The propensity or disposition for public ills exists intrinsically in the weakness of each mortal. . . . The free rein of conscience brought behind it a love for license and political independence. A phantasm was engendered among the dregs of impiety and personal pride, a phantasm that came to be called philosophy, but which was rather the destruction of true philosophy, and this formidable spectre [was] propagated and expanded in the superficial depravity of a number of fanatics. . . . In the judgment of Plato, philosophy was nothing but a love for truth and the exercise of virtue. And, it is quite certain that if virtue and knowledge are united and tightly embraced in those who govern, nothing will be done that is not in accord with the rules of justice and utility, both public and private.[16]

These same ideas on the function of government appear in another work from the same period, the "Discurso sobre el amor de la patria" ("Discourse Concerning Love of Country"), an address that Forner delivered before the Patriotic Society of Seville in 1794. This speech is of particular interest, for it shows his reactions to the French Revolution. In 1794 Forner was actively engaged in aiding the refugees of that revolution and his personal experience surely reinforced his approval of an enlightened monarchy and instilled in him a distrust of democracy.

In what part of the globe, in what barbarian or savage region is saintly virtue not solemnized? Even evildoers themselves recognize in virtue the cement of human happiness, because they know that without helping one another, without coming to one another's aid, without mutually favoring one another, they would degenerate into wild beasts, since each man is by nature incapable of improving himself [without the aid of others]. . . .[17] In order to be happy, a nation must discard any idea that separates its citizens from love of country. If the existence of this corruption becomes possible in a nation, ruin is not far away. The state of war is destructive, and egoism by its very nature is nothing but a civil war of interests that fight and reject each other.[18] . . . A democracy is a field of battle in which the ambition of a few fights for the right to subjugate the people, at the cost of inquietude and often the blood and misery of the people themselves.[19] . . . The establishment of societies [characterized by love of country and upright education] calls for the fruitful constitution of a paternalistic government that puts in the hands of its children part of the wealth so that they may benefit from it.[20] . . .Oh, country of heroes, here is the temple of the purest and most sublime glory: man doing good to man.[21]

V *Ideology and Art*

According to Forner, man is a creature characterized by a tendency to pervert his natural balance of reason and instinct. The most interesting thing about this interpretation is its similarity to Forner's theory of art: the ideal of literary art is a perfect correlation between the precepts and inspiration. The artist's innate gift of talent must always be regulated through an application of the rules dictated by the essence of art. Talent has the same weakness as man — the constant tendency to pervert itself by overstepping the boundaries of good taste.

There is a clear relationship between Forner's idea of man as a rational-instinctive being and his concept of good taste as a rational instinct. In his theory of art, he allows for an occasional excessive expression of the instinctive talent. In his concept of man, he does not clearly express a similar idea, but there is a strong implication that the same is true. Since man's inclination toward God is instinctive, and since reason only serves to confirm that instinct, the excessive exercise of instinct is less harmful than exaggerated reason, which leads to the kind of thing that the *philosophes* were doing. In the *Apologetic Oration* Forner says that "art is not for creating great poets and orators; it is only for allowing those who are born as such to avoid the extravagances and to know the path along which they should guide their talents."[22] Most likely, Forner would have been just as prone to say that reason is not for creating great believers; it is only for allowing those who are born as such to avoid extravagances and to know the path along which they should guide their faith. Throughout Forner's examination of literary theory, he indicates that the precepts only serve to confirm what man instinctively feels to be right. In like manner, reason only serves to confirm what his instinct tells him is right. This, I think, is the foundation of all of Forner's thought.

CHAPTER 9

Forner as Dramatist and Dramatic Theorist

I *Drama and Theory*

A LTHOUGH Forner seemed to be more concerned about dramatic art from about 1790 until his death in 1797, he showed
an interest in the theater very early in his career. He submitted his
play, *The Spanish Captive Girl,* to the censor in 1784, and made major statements on drama in the *Letter to Don Ignacio López de Ayala*
(1784) and in the *Reflections of Tomé Cecial* (1786). In 1790
Forner's activities in theater and dramatic criticism increased: he
wrote the "Lorenzo Garrote" letter in defense of Moratín; he
published the "Reflections Concerning the Theater" — part of the
Funeral Rite manuscript — in *La Espigadera* (*The Gleaner*), the
journal directed by his group of friends; and he wrote a play, *The
Enamored Philosopher.* In 1795, Forner devoted almost all his
energy to a campaign to establish a theater in Seville and to the
polemic that followed. The following year, *The Enamored
Philosopher* was produced in Madrid and published with Forner's
preface, the "Apology for the Masses in Relation to Dramatic
Poetry."

There is evidence that Forner wrote a number of plays other than
The Spanish Captive Girl and *The Enamored Philosopher.* Cueto
reports that there were fragments of three plays among the
manuscripts that he consulted: a play called *La vanidad castigada*
(*Vanity Chastised*) and two tragedies, *Motezuma* and *Francisco
Pizarro.* Cueto also quotes from a letter to Forner written by Estala,
who says that another play, *El ateista* (*The Atheist*), could not be
produced for political reasons; and Cueto also says that Forner "left
a play entitled *Los falsos filósofos* (*The False Philosophers*),"[1] and
notes that the first scene of the tragedy *Las vestales* (*The Vestal
Virgins*) is reprinted in the notes to Forner's *Philosophical Discourses*

Concerning Man. According to Cotarelo, *The Gleaner* published a *Tragedia urbana (Urban Tragedy)*, which the journal claimed "in its plot, its situations, its noble and vehement affectations, its elegant and harmonious versification, its invention and denouement, is a tragedy that will bring honor to Spain at some future time."[2] Also, the Library of Congress catalogue indicates that Forner is the Juan Francisco Pastor who wrote *Pablo y Virginia, drama pastoral sacado de la historia que escribió en francés Santiago Bernardino Enrique de Saint-Pierre, puesta en verso y acomodada al teatro español (Paul and Virginia, Pastoral Drama Taken from the History Written in French by Santiago Bernardino Enrique de Saint-Pierre, Put in Verse and Accomodated to the Spanish Theater).*[3]

The only play that Forner published was *The Enamored Philosopher,* and as far as anyone knows he did not preserve the manuscripts of any of his plays. This indicates, I think, that he did not consider his plays to be very good or very important. He did, however, preserve the manuscripts of his writings on dramatic theory and criticism, and most of them were published during his lifetime. His ideas on the theater coincide perfectly with his other concepts of literature. These ideas are presented in their most concise form in the "Reflections Concerning the Theater," the manuscript that Cañizares reads in the *Funeral Rite.*

The theater cannot be viewed with indifference in any nation which desires that the common people acquire an instruction that will overcome the gross ideas of plebeian education and which desires that the arts of imitation flower. . . . There is not now nor has there ever been a wise people whose first steps toward wisdom did not begin with dramatic poetry. . . . The arts that combine entertainment and usefulness are those that gently inspire in peoples the knowledge of that which is best, and spread and propagate good taste in doctrines. And, among these arts, it is indisputable that the principal one is the dramatic, because of its being like a center or point of concurrence in which are joined together all the pleasing arts, to instruct and improve men with the wooings of imitation.[4] . . . The end of theatrical representation has been, from its very origin, to correct and to teach. The vices of the common people are corrected by making them ridiculous; those of high people by the atrocity of their punishment at the hands of that important fate called fortune, for the principle object of this art is to present examples that obligate fleeing from vice and trusting little in grandeur. . . . Dramas are not, and should not be, anything more than parables put into action, natural examples of human life, disenchantments that improve society, painting with verisimilitude what really happens in society.[5]

The theater is the artistic form with the greatest potential because it can most effectively achieve the end of art — teach while delighting. This delightful teaching is achieved by seducing the audience with "imitation": with *natural* examples of human life, with a portrayal of *what really happens* in society. This is a very curious statement, since the neoclassic concept of imitation is based not on an exact portrayal of reality, but on that happy medium between harsh realism and exaggerated idealism. Surely Forner means a portrayal of what *should* really happen in society; or he must mean that the dramatist is very selective about the examples that he uses, and uses only those cases that provide the appropriate object lessons. The object lesson must be presented through situations that appear to be true to life.

In all of Forner's statements on the theater, there is the concept that the audience will necessarily be delighted by the imitation, that it will respond with pleasure to the portrayal of a versimiliar situation on stage simply because it is verisimilar. And, that pleasurable response teaches the audience that what it sees is right. This is related to Forner's ideas about good taste — that rational instinct. The spectator instinctively responds with pleasure to tasteful things presented in a tasteful way, and subjecting that response to rational reflection, he knows that it is right. Good taste begets good taste; a pleasurable response to imitation begets a pleasurable response to imitation.

In Forner's "Reflections Concerning the Theater," one of the most interesting things is his distortion of the Aristotelean concept of catharsis. The purpose of the noble character's punishment is to present a model for action, to mold behavior. This is quite different from the usual interpretation of catharsis, which deals more with the spiritual experience of identification with the character's suffering and thereby experiencing a cleansing of the soul. This distortion is not surprising, however, in the context of Forner's attitude about art as a didactic device with a very direct application. The end of art is to refine man, not in some vague spiritual way, but through providing models for his actions and for his beliefs.

II   *The Uninstructed Public and the Theater*

When Forner presents this idea that the spectator will naturally be pleased by the representation of a verisimilar situation on the stage, he is speaking of a particular kind of spectator. In his other writings on the theater, he concedes that not all men will respond readily to this kind of play. The common herd, the *vulgo*, is susceptible to being entertained by those extravagant distortions of reality typical of the seventeenth century. Even Cañizares realizes this as he reads the "Reflections Concerning the Theater," and his contrition is so great that he tries to tear up his own plays. These are the plays that fail to maintain that happy mediium which characterizes all works of good taste.

Forner deals with the problem of the common people and the theater in the preface to *The Enamored Philosopher*. He points out that the common people are unable to distinguish between what is and what is not appropriate in a play, between what is and what is not a temperate, verisimilar representation. They are not to blame for their lack of ability, however, for "they were never guilty of anything except of not having stoned to death the first [dramatists] who accustomed them to liking nonsense. But in the common man there is no rule of discernment other than that of pleasure. And since monsters delight just the same as imitation, the common man could hardly know whether the pleasure that he felt as he saw such irregularity was born of a rational principle or of a mechanical sentiment independent of reflection and of judgment."[6]

The common man must be instructed, so that he will be able to discern between the appropriate and the inappropriate in the theater. The theater itself is the best tool for instructing him, for it is the one art form that reaches the uninstructed general public. And, because the good play is based on the idea of imitation, the play also instructs the common man in what is appropriate in life itself. The theater has two important, closely related functions: it refines the common man as a member of society and it refines his artistic sensibility. Thus, dramatic imitation does not consist simply of "painting with verisimilitude what really happens in society" as Forner says in the *Funeral Rite*. Rather, it is a selective process of painting with verisimilitude the things that really happen in society *if* they are the things that should really happen in society. There is always an attitude of confirming those things that match the ideal, and condemning or ignoring the things that do not match the ideal.

That comment in the *Funeral Rite* was really directed against those plays that presented gross exaggerations of human behavior for the purpose of entertaining the general public, those things for which the dramatists should have been stoned to death. Forner talks about that kind of play, and about the common man's unrefined taste, in the *Letter to Ayala*, as he defends his own play about the captive girl. He gives a list of all those absurd exaggerations and declares himself innocent of propagating them: "I thought that the act alone of not presenting those absurdities in the theater was of some merit, seeing the distraction found in the common people; but now I see that the censors do not want the common people to lose sight of the frivolous objects that distract them."[7]

That was in 1784, and again in 1786 Forner (as Tomé Cecial) expresses a similar idea when he defends Cervantes as a dramatist and attacks Huerta's ideas "for the benefit of the ignorant common people."[8] The general public must be instructed, and "among satirical works there is none more skillful nor more instructive than the play. Its school is imitating bad actions in such a way that they become ridiculous, to make them despicable and abhorrent. The common people have no school other than the theater, and in a good play they are given lessons that they do not receive in their education and perhaps do not understand, or disregard, in the temples."[9] The same idea appears again in Forner's letter published in 1790 under the pseudonym of Lorenzo Garrote, in defense of Moratín's *The Old Man and the Maiden*.

These men [who have criticized Moratín] believe that they have exercised the role of comic writers if they have enthralled the *uninstructed public* with characters doing whatever in whatever way. They refuse to understand that the *uninstructed public* is entertained an infinite number of times by boring and ridiculous things, for no reason other than that they are pleased by anything that strikes them in an extraordinary way, even if it strikes with irrationality.[10]

As in all of Forner's literary theory, there are two questions involved in his concept of dramatic art — what should be presented, and in what way it should be presented. The dramatist should present a good lesson, but the way in which he presents it is just as much a lesson in propriety as is the lesson itself. Forner talks about both questions in the *Letter to Ayala:*

Nor does the censor find a *good example* in the *Captive Girl*. A drama in which are manifest in a practical way the evils to which a man abandons himself when he leaves the best religion of all; a drama in which the crimes are always accompanied by an interior accusation and the accusation of remorse; a drama in which the character of a totally virtuous woman stands out in contrast to the vices portrayed. This is not a drama of *good example* for the professor of poetics [Ayala]. Does the good censor know the dramatic mode of persuasion? He gives very few indications of it.[11]

Forner's comment about a good example presented "in a practical way" has two meanings. The lesson must be presented in a practical way characterized by good taste in order to be acceptable to the educated spectator with refined taste. Also, the dramatist must find a practical way of appealing to the uneducated public so that he can instruct them. He must find a way to hold their attention without overstepping the limits of good taste. This is, in fact, another expression of Forner's concept of the happy medium. The dramatist must make some compromises in order to find a balance between what the public wants to see and what the dramatist wants them to see. Forner claims that he has done just this in *The Spanish Captive Girl*. In the *Letter to Ayala*, Forner gives the censor a preview of the article that will appear in newspapers throughout Europe reporting Ayala's unjust censure of Forner's play:

From Madrid they write the following anecdote, which shows that there is someone in Spain who wants to contribute to the improvement of the theater, and that there are also some ridiculous geniuses who make it impossible. Monsieur Ayala is charged with censuring the dramas that are to be produced. A young man who was awarded a prize by the Spanish Academy in the year 1782 presented a play for censoring. If it is not completely good, it is infinitely better than all the hypocrisies seen on the stage every day. It observes art with all the scrupulosity that can be applied to a complicated action. It seems that the author has tried to unite regularity and that complication of plot still very pleasing to the Spaniards, in order to insinuate good taste without displeasing them with simplicity, which they cannot bear. In truth, there is no better way to begin achieving that which is desired, because by pleasing the audience, by satisfying them with what gives them pleasure, absurd improprieties can gradually be eliminated.[12]

After this article, Forner again declares: "I tried to observe the principal laws of dramatic art, joining them to an involved action which I myself invented, to accommodate myself in part to the style of our theater and to the vulgar taste."[13] Forner is at least realistic in his attempt to improve the taste of the public. He makes certain concessions to them, but tries to stay within the boundaries of good taste, as represented by the "principal laws of dramatic art." Forner also asks: "What are the fundamental rules? The unities, verisimilitude, decorum, characters, customs, diction; the rest, Mr. Censor, depends on the arbitrariness or taste of each individual."[14] One wonders what Forner means by "the rest," since the characteristics that he has enumerated seem to cover every possible ingredient of a play. He probably means the specific way in which the rules are applied, but he fails to say so. He also fails to explain any of those terms, and he even shows a certain amount of disdain about having to elaborate on the rules, as if everyone should be able to recognize their application in a play without resorting to that kind of analysis.

In Forner's dramatic theory, then, there are two basic principles. The play should present appropriate content which edifies and entertains by presenting a moral lesson that delights the audience; and the play should present that lesson in an appropriate way, tastefully, so that it does not offend the refined spectator by catering unnecessarily to the uneducated, or bore the uninstructed spectator by disregarding his taste in theater. This is Forner's theory, and it is important to consider whether he practiced this theory in his own dramatic compositions. Since Forner often observed that critics find it very easy to criticize the things that they themselves are incapable of doing, it is revealing to see whether Forner was capable of doing the things that he encouraged others to do and condemned others for not doing.

III   *The Imperfect Play:* The Spanish Captive Girl

The Spanish Captive Girl, rejected by the censor López de Ayala in 1784, was never published. The manuscript has disappeared, perhaps destroyed by Forner himself, since he refers to it as "my abortive attempt, which has concerned me very little."[15] The *Letter to Ayala* contains a great deal of information about the plot of the play, as Forner defends it in detail and says enough about it to give a fairly complete idea of what kind of play it was. Forner's defense implies that Ayala had said that it was preachy, unrealistic, and even immoral in some of its material. In other words, it was inappropriate both in the material that it presented and in the way that it presented that material.

Since this propriety of material and technique is the fundamental tenet of Forner's dramatic theory, the length and sarcasm of the *Letter to Ayala* is quite understandable. In retrospect, Forner's anger was productive, for it resulted in a detailed analysis of his own play, an analysis that helps us to understand further his dramatic theory and practice.

And so, since it suits you to call the impassioned reasonings of my Captive Girl *sermons*, it is not worthy of being presented? And so, since you find inverisimilar one of the most common things in the world — an old man furiously in love with a young girl — my poor *Isabela* is to be excluded from the theater? . . . You told me face to face that it is not verisimilar for an old renegade to force a young man in his power to also become a renegade in order to make impossible the young man's love for *Isabela*, and thus to make her his own. . . . Do the forces of love not go far beyond that? . . . Neither do you want an old man to fall in love with a young girl; and, because it is discovered at the end of the drama that she is his daughter, you say with candid simplemindedness that it is dishonorable for a father to be enamored of his daughter. . . . Tell me, sir: does that father continue soliciting her when he knows that she is in fact his daughter? No. Nothing of the sort. Rather, that recognition transforms in one blow all the designs of the father and arouses in him the pure sentiments of nature, making a man of the monster that he was. . . .

You mainly emphasize the tender and affectionate scene in which Isabela sees that her lover has just become a Mohammedan and tries to dissuade him and restore him to his first religion. And to make her forceful argument look ridiculous, you give it the name of *sermon*. How well the censor understands the talent of theatrical situations. This is the situation in which Isabela finds herself at that moment: A renegade [is] in love with a young captive girl serving in his house; he knows that this girl and a young man — another captive serving in his house (whom he calls son although he really is not) — have tenderly fallen in love; he tries to make the young man become a Mohammedan in order to separate him from the love of the girl and thus facilitate his own designs on her. To this end, he forces him to suffer four years of violent and vile work, martyrs him in a thousand ways, and . . . finally succeeds. The young man, in despair, . . . abandons his religion one day (which is the day on which the drama's action begins) according to the wishes of the old renegade, who has told him from his childhood that he is his father, though he is not. The girl sees her lover dressed as a Moor and, shocked, asks him what is going on. The lover, seized with despair, reveals everything to her.

Now then, let the professor of poetics tell me: . . . what should she do and say? Reason dictates that she should dissuade him . . . [and] she does this precisely because of the effect of the situation in which she finds herself. And the censor calls this a *sermon?* When a woman finds herself in need of restoring her lover to a religion that he has abandoned, can she not speak to him of the merit of the religion that he has abandoned?[16]

The main points of Forner's rebuttal, then, are that the material is appropriate, because it is verisimilar; and that the way in which he has incorporated the "sermons" into the play is equally appropriate, because the "impassioned reasonings" of Isabela are justified by the dramatic situation. Forner's plot summary indicates that the play was very similar to the kind of dramatic works that he often criticized. The dramatic device of plot complications through mistaken identity was very common in the seventeenth-century theater, and was carried over into the most popular dramatic productions of the eighteenth century. Most likely, Forner's justification for what he had done — achieved a happy medium between the public taste and his own idea of good theater — was an attempt to conceal his own error. It probably made the play sound better than it really was.

However, the way in which Forner turns this kind of play into a didactic, moralizing drama is very interesting. Forner used that popular technique of confused identities to provide a framework for his "sermons." And they probably were indeed sermons, for his comments about Christianity as the best religion and Mohammedism as "an abominable religion" indicate the doctrinal content of the play. Forner used the mistaken identity as a kind of deus ex machina that transformed the "monster" with amazing rapidity and all too suddenly restored him to "the pure sentiments of nature." It was, most likely, a very bad play which combined the worst of two dramatic worlds — the complicated plot devices of the seventeenth-century theater and the exaggerated didacticism of the eighteenth-century stage.

IV *The Perfect Play:* The Enamored Philosopher

In 1796, Forner succeeded in having his *School for Friendship, or The Enamored Philosopher* produced in Madrid through the help of his friend Estala. Since the text of *The Spanish Captive Girl* does not exist, it is difficult to make comparisons between that play and *The Enamored Philosopher*. However, compared to Forner's plot summary of that first play, *The Enamored Philosopher* seems to be a much better example of the kind of play that Forner applauds in his theoretical writings. While it is not particularly outstanding, it does indicate that he might have been rather good at this kind of theater if he had continued developing his ability in this area.

In *The Enamored Philosopher*, Silvestre is forcing his sister, Inés, to marry the Marqués de la Espina, a wealthy and prominent nobleman. Inés is in love with another young man, Fernando, and her maid, Benita, suggests a remedy to the situation: convince Felipe, a "man of mature age, very rich, extremely prudent and honorable, but of such rare and extravagant talent that he lives wrapped up in his books, ignorant of the world that he scorns,"[17] to pretend to be in love with Inés. Silvestre will be so impressed with him that he will agree to let Inés marry him, then Felipe will step aside and leave her to Fernando. They agree to the plan, and Fernando approaches Felipe with it. He finds him shut away in his study, speaking about women as "mortal poison for one who aspires to preserve the severe character of virtue."[18] Out of friendship for Fernando, Felipe agrees, and Silvestre is enchanted with the philosopher, particularly when he finds out that Felipe will not ask for a dowry. The situation becomes complicated, however, when Felipe finds Inés to be a delightful female indeed. He realizes the errors of his ways: "When one runs into an Inés, when virtue and beauty are brothers, I am persuaded that one who lives as a hermit without having a vocation is not right."[19]

When Fernando realizes what has happened, he agrees to let Inés decide between the two men, for she will choose the one who better combines wisdom and virtue. Meanwhile, Felipe gets a summons to court, for the jealous Espina has accused him of offending his honor. Fernando, Inés, and Luisa (Inés' sister) go to the authorities and Luisa talks to Espina while the judge is hidden, listening to their conversation. Espina admits that he has done all this to heal his wounded pride, and the judge frees Felipe. Fernando gives up Inés, saying that it was wrong for them to have used Felipe in this way, causing him harm and breaking his heart. Inés agrees to marry Felipe in order to reward his virtuous act of helping them, but Felipe refuses and delivers a discourse on virtue and friendship: "My consolation will be the fortuitous happiness of these two souls who repay with virtue the desires of a friend that loves them. And so that they will exercise that virtue, let them always bear this lesson, so that they may be a lustre and an honor to their country."[20]

The Enamored Philosopher fulfills Forner's theoretical formula for the perfect play. It is pleasantly amusing at times, particularly in the portrayal of the philosopher who hates women and has closed himself off from the world. It teaches through the examples that it presents — through the kind of characters that are portrayed and through the moralizing content of their "set speeches." Inés is presented as a woman who combines beauty and virtue in perfect balance. Fernando is the incarnation of friendship, selflessness, and moderation in all things. And Felipe, the philosopher, is first an example of perverted values, his reason completely negating his instinctive passion; then, he serves as an example of passion overwhelming reason as he falls in love with Inés; and finally, he achieves a perfect balance between the two parts of his constitution, passion and reason. In fact, it is his achieving this balance that provides the resolution of the play in a manner satisfactory to all. Fernando and Inés are allowed to marry, Silvestre realizes the error of his greed, Espina is censured for his unattractive behavior, and Felipe has found good friends and has come out of his self-imposed alienation from society.

The Enamored Philosopher is a good example of the neoclassic ideal of the *utile dulci* in two ways. The lesson of the play's content presents a model for human behavior, and the play itself, as a work of art, is an example of what a play should be. Both as appropriate action in society, and as a representation of that appropriate action on the stage in an appropriate way, the play fulfills Forner's theoretical prerequisites for useful dramatic literature. This is not to say that it is a particularly good play, because it is not. It has a contrived air about it, mainly because Forner makes everything happen too fast, without adequate preparation. The changes in the philosopher's attitudes toward society are not very convincing, and the characters have a tendency to slip into caricature. Yet the play is a good example of eighteenth-century Spanish theater. Forner has followed all the rules and come up with a play that is amusing and didactic in a temperate, inoffensive way.

In the "Apology for the Masses" that serves as a preface to the published edition of the play, Forner talks about *The Enamored Philosopher* in terms of its adherence to the dramatic precepts. Here, as before, he approves of the regularity imposed by those precepts but also scorns the need to subject his play to this kind of stingy examination.

The play of the philosopher is not a monster, in spite of what we have been led to believe by these dictatorial pedants who think that they have sufficient capacity to perceive the merit or lack of merit in works of ingenuity just because they have mechanically decorated four little rules of poetics. That it is not a monster can be proven very easily if we want to get into the pedantic boredom of putting it to the test of the rules and demonstrate, through this application, that it is extremely regular in its action, in its continuity, and in its unraveling of plot.[21]

Later in the "Apology for the Masses" Forner indicates the appropriate function of the precepts: "The rules will be of little use to cold and frozen talents, and the great and vehement talents cannot submit themselves completely to the servitude of strict regularity.

Without this tolerance, we cannot expect a restoration of the theater."[22] Forner's theory of drama coincides with his concept of art in general: the rules are there to prevent inspiration from exceeding the limits of good taste. An occasional excess, however, is necessary for the really inspired writer and often can have great artistic value if it is not too pronounced. The rules have no real value other than as a kind of safeguard. As Forner has said before, the precepts will not make an artist.

And there is that other concession to a less rigid application of the rational precepts: too much regularity will create a kind of theater that holds no appeal for the masses. It is necessary to cater to their tastes to some extent in order to seduce them into gradually refining their sensibilities. As Forner sees it, this is the aim of the popularization of neoclassic art: to improve the quality of the average man by raising him slowly but deliberately to a more refined level. Only the theater can do that, for it is the only school that has the potential for remedying their plebeian education.

CHAPTER 10

Forner as Linguistic Purist

I   A *History of Corruption: The* Funeral Rite for the Castilian Language

THE general consensus of criticism has awarded Forner a relatively insignificant place in the canon of Spanish literature. Until the publication of two different editions of *The Grammarians* in 1970, the only major work by Forner available in a readily accessible edition was the *Funeral Rite for the Castilian Language*, which appeared first in 1871 in the *Biblioteca de Autores Españoles* and then in 1925 in the *Clásicos Castellanos* series. This scarcity of Forner editions is both the result and the cause of the prevailing attitude toward his work. Since literary criticism obviously deals with literature, it has looked for works of literary significance; and it has found literary significance only in the *Funeral Rite*, and only to the extent that it is interpreted as a defense of purism in the literature of Spain.

The basic premise of the *Funeral Rite* is indeed that point of view, and statements about linguistic purism are scattered throughout many of Forner's other works. Forner, however, was a man of contradictions, and the *Funeral Rite* does not bear out its claim as a treatise on pure linguistic expression, at least not in the way that it seems to at first. Forner was a purist in questions concerning language, but for reasons very different from the obvious ones. The frequency with which I have referred to the *Funeral Rite* in my discussions of Forner's other concerns indicates that this work deals with many things other than purism in language. The *Funeral Rite* is developed entirely through a motif of dialogues on language, but that motif is only a device for creating a compendium of all Forner's other concerns.

However, there are several extensive passages in the *Funeral Rite* that do deal specifically with the language itself. One of these is a discourse delivered by Cervantes to explain the presence of the *bustuarios*, those who must watch the burning of the body as punishment for their role in the assassination of the Castilian language.

Apollo has decreed this punishment for the assassins of our language, and he has singled out the semi-Gauls because they are incorrigible and because they have effected the death of the respectable matron using the filthiest and most heinous illness possible. They worked at it furiously and desperately. She saw herself debilitated first with the horrible persecution with which the *culteranos* almost provoked her death in my time; then with the countless martyrdoms that she received from the *equivoquistas* and *conceptistas* later; then with the immense and extravagant weight of adornments put on her by those who thought that they were beautifying her — the adornments with which the preachers and novelists of this your century almost drowned her. Without defenders or patrons to help her, in vain she resisted the insults of the Gallicized rabble and finally contracted their illness. The pain reached its extreme, and, harrassed more and more by the fury of the corrupters, she fled her country and arrived here, where she died in the arms of that respectable old man [Mayans] that you saw a little while ago. Since he was her last and only defender in his country, he has been the one to receive the last breath from the lips of that great and generous soul. It is time that you saw her. Come and lament your misfortune in hers, seeing yourselves deprived of the best instrument of your ideas.[1]

In Cervantes' history of the crime, the causes of corruption are clear: the literary movements that created a complicated use of language to excess — the *conceptismo* and *culteranismo* of the seventeenth century, the same complication of language in the prosists of the eighteenth century, and the use of Gallicisms. All these excesses, which were offered as adornments, in fact obscured the natural beauty and clarity of the language.

Later there is another long discourse on language, a history of the development of Castilian, delivered by Villegas. His historical analysis of the fortunes and misfortunes of the language is as follows:

1. In the sixteenth century, the Castilian language was at her pinnacle of eloquence and beauty, and was constructed on the ruins of the languages spoken by all the invaders, dominated by the most noble characteristics of the most noble language, Latin. The regularity demanded by the precepts was cultivated through Greek erudition and through the Graeco-Roman poetic style of Boscán, Garcilaso,

and Hurtado de Mendoza. The historians added the eloquence of
their refined rhetorical style.

2. The period of Philip III (1598 - 1621) was characterized by gran-
diloquence and majesty, particularly in the work of Cervantes,
Villegas himself, and Lope de Vega.

3. The reign of Philip IV (1621 - 65) added the luxuriance and splendor of the court in the works of writers like Quevedo and Calderón.

4. During the reign of Charles II (1665 - 1700) the language experienced a decline, since "language follows the fortune and
customs of empires."[2]

5. The eighteenth century received the language "languid, made
ugly by a new barbarity, corrupted and eternally weighted down
with its own vices and those of others, which is the greatest extreme
of corruption that the use of language can reach."[3]

This new barbarity, the combination of the native vices and the
vices of others, consists of excesses in prose and the Gallicisms
pointed out by Cervantes in his analysis of the causes of corruption.
Forner's characters always tend to place more blame on those "vices
of others," the Gallicisms. After Villegas ends his history of the
language, he adds some comments to the effect that the French
language has become the repository of all knowledge; thus the whole
world wants to emulate the French. The Spaniards, in copying their
ideas from the French, have also copied their locutions without
realizing it, mainly because of an abysmal ignorance of their own
language.

Thus, in looking for the source of this tendency to Gallicize the
language, Forner suggests a relationship between the language and
the content, the ideas expressed by that language. In his evaluation
of the literature and language of the mystic writers, Forner goes
much farther with this idea. Because of the prominence of Luis de
Granada, Luis de León, and Teresa de Jesús in the literature of
mysticism, "among the modern languages, Castilian is the most appropriate for speaking with the Maker and Supreme Arbiter of the
universe. . . ."[4] This relationship between language and content is
again expressed as the South American savages parade in front of the
bier, thanking the Castilian language for having saved them from

their pagan customs. This is accompanied by a defense of Spain's participation in the conquest of the New World, and Apollo himself declares that "no one, except one who loves barbarity, will consider it a crime to obligate the barbarian that he not be one, when his barbarity is pernicious and ignoble to the human race."[5] This too is a rebuttal to Masson, who went to great lengths to point out the cruelty of the Spaniards in that venture. But the savages come along with the mystics, and the implication is clear: they are thanking the *language*, not the nation, for their salvation, because the language is the instrument of the doctrines that rescued them from their paganism.

It is clear that there is much more to Forner's ideal of linguistic purity than there seems to be on the surface. Throughout the *Funeral Rite*, the principal thrust of this ideal is the censure of any Gallicizing of the Castilian language. Mayans swears that he "tried to maintain and propagate the propriety and purity of our language at a time when nothing but gobbledegook was spoken"[6] and then he engages in some ironic self-criticism: "I know very well that my writings are used very little today, and that it is my fault, since I did not manage to Frenchify them . . . . I wrote a *Castilian Rhetoric*, and instead of giving examples of French authors to show the elegance of our language, I had the stupidity to make use of examples from pure, chaste, elegant Spanish authors."[7] Aminta offers the opinion that the epic and the tragedy require a particularly eloquent language such as Castilian, but that "a perverse envy of imitating that which is not in any way enviable has reduced us to throwing out completely the poetic style of the tragedy. And all because in France, the country whose language lacks that style, they put tragedies in rimed prose, since this is their only kind of poetry."[8] Apollo goes around turning into frogs all those who translated French works and thereby corrupted the language with the inevitable Gallicisms, and Arcadio delivers a discourse damning the Spanish prose writers who imitated French rhetorical works:

The bad thing is that, although the structure of our language is infinitely more beautiful, more eloquent, more ample, more varied, and more flexible than that of the very exact and therefore very arid, indocile, and monotonous French dialect, . . . they have transferred its locutions and expressions [to Castilian], some out of ignorance, others out of servile novelty. This is because they think that for eloquence, the grandeur or excellence of the things that are said is all that is necessary, and not the expression with which they are said.[9]

This is related to Villegas' suggestion that the Castilian language became Gallicized through a kind of accident, that the Spaniards inadvertently imitated the French language as they were emulating the ideology of the French Enlightenment. One of the causes was the Spaniards' ignorance of their own language. Another cause, which Forner does not state explicitly but often implies, is his concept that there is a close relationship between a given language and the content that it is accustomed to expressing. Just as Castilian offers the greatest possibilities for communicating with God because of its experience in mystic literature, Castilian perhaps is unable to express the ideology of the French because it has never been used to deal with that kind of material.

This concept is, to be sure, a little far-fetched, since the Castilian in the eighteenth century was quite well equipped to deal with the ideas of Enlightenment philosophy. But Forner is very convinced of this idea that his language is insufficiently prepared to express certain things, and that that insufficiency has been resolved by the use of Gallicisms. Through his insistence on this idea, Forner inadvertently begins to remove his disguise: his objections to Gallic influence in the Castilian language are really objections to the corruption of Spanish thought with the ideas of the French Enlightenment.

Although Forner does not ever clearly express this concept of language, he is quite persistent in suggesting it. The only other work devoted almost exclusively to questions of language is *The Featherless Crow*, and there the same ideas appear, along with others that clarify his concept of the appropriate use of language.

II   *Ideology and the Masses*: The Featherless Crow

The Featherless Crow, published in 1795, is an attack on Vargas' *Declamation Against the Abuses Introduced Into Castilian*, and represents one more contradiction in Forner's career. The *Declamation* is a strong condemnation of French influence in the Castilian language and a charge to the king to purify that "best instrument" of the ideas of the Spaniards. It is curious that Forner would attack a book that censures just what he deplores, but there are other things about Vargas' dissertation on language that provoked the ire of Forner. The main point of *The Featherless Crow* is Forner's contention that Vargas' book is a plagiarism of Mayans' *Origins of the Castilian Language*, and Forner reprints passages from the two works in parallel columns to prove it.

This charge of plagiarism is not of much interest, but Forner also makes a number of comments about language that amplify what he said in the *Funeral Rite* about linguistic expertise as a direct result of linguistic exercise.

Here is a truth that the crowish dissertator will not dare deny: that the Castilian language has not prospered — has not reached as great a degree of abundance and propriety — as it would have if learned men had dedicated themselves to using it to explain all the sciences and the arts. For that is a truth that will penetrate the eyes of any beginner in Spanish literature, piercing him with totally irrefutable testimonies. Now then: if a language is not cultivated in the most serious subjects, in those which are most useful and most important to rationality and to life, what follows is: that language is looked on with disdain and consecrated solely to frivolous things and to the readings of the common man. From being looked on with disdain comes the very easy propensity to become corrupted; and corruption brings with it the universal distortion of good taste in speaking, or, shall we say, the adulteration of eloquence, which is the organ of literary beauties.[10]

This, then, is a much clearer expression of the concept of language than that presented in the *Funeral Rite*. In *The Featherless Crow* Forner is talking primarily about expository writing and oratory, and he suggests that the failure to deal with the right subjects in those prose forms has led to a corruption of the language. The progress of that cause is clear: the language fails to deal with the right material; that failure elicits disdain; that disdain paves the way for corruption; that corruption distorts good taste in the use of language.

Forner is not suggesting that the Spaniards have not dealt with those serious, useful, important subjects; but rather, that they have not dealt with them in Spanish. Those subjects have been explored extensively by the Spaniards, but in Latin. This is a response to Vargas' charge that Spanish was corrupted by seventeenth-century attempt to refine the language by limiting its vocabulary to words of Latin origin. Forner's rebuttal to Vargas' accusation clarifies further his concept of the relationship between language and content.

. . . Between a language's not reaching the perfection that it could achieve, through lack of cultivation, and its corrupting itself after being perfected, there lies a great distance. This distance is the thing that escaped the perspicacity of our thieving bird. . . . Those who attributed the decline of our language to the mania of writing everything in Latin . . . did not mean that this mania was influential in the corruption of the Castilian language. Rather, they meant that the Castilian language, through lying in unjust scorn, did not become enriched or enlightened with the beauties of which its genius is capable . . . . Agreed, then: the use of Latin did not influence the corruption of Castilian, rather it contributed to its decline, its poverty, and its dismantling . . . .[11]

Forner censures Vargas for his proclamation that "the particular dialects (as he [Vargas] calls the vulgar languages of all nations) should be used in the histories of each people and in their poetry, but everything that is treated for the benefit of the understanding and for the benefit of society in general should be executed and deposited in the form in which it can easily be found by everyone (that is, in the Latin tongue)."[12] This idea that Latin should be the language of all significant knowledge is very repugnant to Forner. Although Forner always exhibits a certain disdain for the masses, his solution to the problem of the unrefined masses is not to ignore them, but to educate them. This is important in explaining Forner's concern for linguistic purity and clarity of expression. Because language is an instrument for the expression of ideas, it must be clear in order to make those ideas accessible to everyone. Also, the refinement of that instrument is as important as the ideas themselves in the propagation of good taste.

Forner's consistently paternalistic attitude toward the masses does not, however, permit a mongrelization of knowledge. He is concerned with refining the common man, not catering to his base inclinations and tastes. This is evident in his discussion of the proper use of Latin and the vulgar tongue:

The arts and sciences solidly and judiciously treated are the source of good taste . . . . If a nation is to have good poetry, it must know how to esteem it; and it will not esteem it if it does not know it; and it will not know it if it does not possess correct ideas of things; and these correct ideas are not acquired through inspired science. Rather, they are obtained through the reading of classic books and through the elementary knowledge of the *good* and the *beautiful* . . . . If we take from the masses the instruments for their rational and civil instruction, they will be left with nothing but their inclination to walk on all fours . . . . Everything from which the people can draw rational, moral, and civil utility should be written in the vulgar tongue; and all profound discussions, examinations, and tentative pronouncements concerning the sciences and their progress should be written in Latin. In these, learned men work toward improving and advancing the sciences, but the fruits of these improvements and advances belong by right to all men, toward whom they are directed.[13]

The learned men should conduct their examinations, their disputes, their tentative reasonings in Latin, but they should then make accessible to everyone the results of their investigations. It need not be pointed out how paternalistic this is. Vargas had suggested that Latin was the language accessible to everyone, and Forner insists that the spoken language of a given country is the language accessible to everyone. The different orientation of the two writers is obvious. To Forner, "everyone" means *everyone*, and therein lies the danger. And therein lies another explanation for his objections to the activities of the French. Through the multitude of dictionaries and encyclopedias, the French were attempting to enlighten everyone with ideas to which Forner was vehemently opposed. And this explains Forner's objections to similar activities on the part of Spaniards. Sempere's *Library of the Best Writers of the Reign of Charles III* and Huerta's *Spanish Theater* were attempts at something like a popular encyclopedia. Although their ideas were not so heretical as those of the "transpyrenaics," those projects struck Forner as attempts to propagate erroneous ideas. The *Funeral Rite*, in fact, was a kind of encyclopedic attempt to correct all the misconceptions of his unfortunate contemporaries.

III *A Compendium of Universal Knowledge: The* Funeral Rite

As I have noted throughout this study, there is evidence that Forner continued refining the *Funeral Rite* until his death in 1797. It is quite appropriate that this supposed dissertation on linguistic purity should be the masterpiece of this man of contradictions, for it is his most contradictory work. In one way or another, it embraces every important aspect of his career. The *Funeral Rite* incorporates all the roles in which Forner cast himself — polemist and satirist, literary theorist and critic, defender of the faith, dramatic theorist and playwright — and all these ultimately depend on his concept of language. Yet only a very small part of the *Funeral Rite* deals specifically with linguistic expression.

The same is true of Forner's work as a whole. There are hundreds and hundreds of references to the corruption of the language through Gallicisms and through excessive adornments, but there is not a single case of clear, precise textual criticism to support his observations. The *Funeral Rite* is filled with material about Castilian eloquence, the history of the development of the language, the claims that the poetry and prose of one period is more beautiful and

elegant than those of another period, but all of this is offered without
a single quotation from the sources. This, I think, 'is adequate
evidence that Forner had only a vague idea of what he was talking
about and that he knew nothing about textual criticism. He based
everything that he said on his own very subjective opinions, and he
never bothered to verify his observations and theories.

The *Funeral Rite*, with its primary motif of the purity of linguistic
expression, is an enormous contradiction. Forner purports to be saying one thing when he is really saying something else. The motif of
linguistic purism is actually a metaphor for another kind of purism.
Apollo deciphers the metaphor when he admonishes the spectators
to grieve the death of "the best instrument for the expression of your
ideas." The principal function of language is the expression of ideas,
and the unusual amount of attention that Forner gives to vague
pronouncements about the quality of linguistic expression is the
result of the importance that he sees in the ideas himself.

Forner was, first of all, a "philosopher", in the sense in which he
used that term when he said that poets should be philosophers.
Forner saw himself as a filter through which all the knowledge of
mankind would pass and be purified. Many of his works have the air
of a decantation of knowledge on a particular subject, a definitive expression of some body of material cleansed of all its impurities. The
most notable examples are the *Apologetic Oration*, the *Preservative
Against Atheism*, his treatises on history and law, and, of course,
the *Funeral Rite for the Castilian Language*. The end of this
"philosophical" activity was education, in the Fornerian sense of the
word — education with a very clear purpose: the perfection of
society through the establishment of a universal good taste.

Forner's literary criticism also has this purpose: to create a universal good taste by purifying literature and by censuring the critics
who do not work toward the same goal. The close proximity of this
literary criticism to his comments about linguistic purity is evident at
the end of *The Featherless Crow*, as Forner justifies his attack on
Vargas y Ponce:

> But, finally, if I have wasted time and oil on censuring a pamphlet filled
> with such frivolous things, *cui bono?* What benefit could this have to the
> progress of knowledge? The only important utility offered by this genre of
> works is the attempt to prevent the trappings of ignorance, so that in the
> evaluation of talents the fatuous ones will not be confused with the sound
> ones. And this, Ipnocausto discharged marvelously in these few pages that
> he scribbled. Let us thank him for what he wrote, and for what he refrained

from writing. The former, because he gave the uninstructed a useful disenchantment; and the latter, because he spared intelligent men boredom and nausea.[14]

Since everything that Forner censured in Vargas' work had to do with ideas about language, and the summary of his attack is a dissertation on usefulness and knowledge, it is obvious that the relationship between language and knowledge is very close. The same is true in the *Funeral Rite*, in which the motif of linguistic purity draws together all the ideas about literature and its efficacy in the lives of men and in the society that binds them together.

This is further indication that Forner was never very clear about the distinctions between language, artistic form, and content. From the *Comparison of the Eclogues* to his last work there is a failure to make those distinctions. What is said and the way that it is said always tend to become one and the same. Even the very specific comments about linguistic purity participate in this confusion of terms. Forner's frequent complaints about Gallicisms in the language are based on Forner's abhorrence for anything French, and this is the result of his attitude toward French ideology, not toward the French language itself. The question becomes even more complicated by Forner's idea that the language and the ideas expressed in that language are somehow inseparable. Thus, French ideology has a tendency to "taint" the language itself, and Gallicizing Castilian seems to imply Gallicizing Spanish ideology.

The most outstanding contradiction in Forner's activities as a writer is his criticism of others for doing the very things that he does over and over. The only logical explanation for this is found in *The Featherless Crow*, in his distinction between the proper use of Latin and the vulgar languages. When he states that Latin is suitable for those profound studies of science, but the vulgar languages should be used to propagate the fruits of those labors, he reveals one of the foundations of his ideology. Forner had two standards, one for the enlightened few and another for those who needed to be enlightened. Only a very small part of Forner's writings was directed toward the unenlightened masses — his theater. Everything else was addressed to the men who participated in creating literature or criticizing literature. Thus, when he talks about calumny and malediction as destroying the bonds of society, then practices that same calumny and malediction, he is not contradicting himself. He feels, I think, that his polemical activities are valid because all the participants are members of the same class — the enlightened or those who erroneously consider themselves to be enlightened. The calumny and vile attacks can only be constructive, for they have the noble purpose of destroying the false teachers.

This attitude is part of Forner's paternalism toward the masses. He felt that it was his duty to oversee the kind of teachers that the masses would be subjected to. His polemical activities would not have the ultimate effect of disrupting the social bonds that make man happy; rather, they would finally improve those bonds by eliminating bad influences on the public taste. This attitude coincides with his support of censorship. It is significant that Forner was such a strong defender of censorship even though he often was the victim of the censors. The *Grammarians* episode, the rejection of *The Spanish Captive Girl*, the two years that the censor took to approve the *Philosophical Discourses*, his failure to get the *Funeral Rite* published, all must have been detrimental to his career. Yet he continued to support government censorship throughout his life. This indicates that he considered himself to be a part of that "Republic of Letters" that had the task of educating society as a whole and accepted the rules of the game — the censorship, the polemical activity, the abuses — all in the interests of society as a whole.

Whether one agrees with Forner's point of view or not, it is important to see that Forner did consider his activities to be magnanimous, in a very paternalistic way. He really believed that the ideology he consistently proposed and defended in his work was for the benefit of mankind. He failed to see the contradiction between his aims and his methods, and he failed to see the faults that marred his own work with amazing consistency.

If we use Forner's method and turn back on him his comments about Iriarte in the "Apology Wrapped in Satire," we could say that "Sánchez and Huerta did the portraits that suited him best." In spite of his noble ideals, he was like "a man attached to a nose" and he was an incorrigible *tuerto*.

Notes and References

Chapter One

1. The historical data not specifically documented in this book are a compilation from two sources: María Jiménez Salas, *Vida y obras de D. Juan Pablo Forner y Segarra* (Madrid: Consejo Superior de Investigaciones Científicas, 1944); and Emilio Cotarelo y Mori, *Iriarte y su época* (Madrid: Est. Tip. "Sucesores de Rivadeneyra," 1897).

2. Andrés Piquer y Arrufat, *Obras póstumas*, ed. Juan Crisóstomo Piquer (Madrid: Ibarra, 1785), p. 211.

3. *Ibid.*, p. 213.

4. *Ibid.*, p. 212.

5. *Ibid.*, p. 213.

6. "Representación de Forner a Floridablanca, 1 de junio de 1783," in Juan Pablo Forner, *Los gramáticos: historia chinesca*, ed. John H. R. Polt (Berkeley: University of California Press, 1970), pp. 239 - 40.

7. Miguel de la Pinta Llorente, "El sentido de la cultura española en el siglo XVIII e intelectuales de la época (Aportaciones inéditas)," *Revista de estudios políticos*, no. 68 (marzo-abril 1953), pp. 110 - 11.

8. Miguel de Cervantes Saavedra, *El viaje del Parnaso*, in *Obras completas*, ed. Angel Valbuena Prat (Madrid: Aguilar, 1956), pp. 65 - 108.

9. *Cismontano*, from the Latin *cismontanus*, means "situated on this side of the mountains" and here refers to the longwinded heroes of the Spanish tragedies written in Forner's time in imitation of the French theater (Juan Pablo Forner, *Exequias de la lengua castellana*, ed. Pedro Sáinz y Rodríguez, Clásicos Castellanos, no. 66 [Madrid: Espasa-Calpe, 1956], p. 36n). All subsequent references to the *Exequias* are to this edition.

10. *Exequias*, pp. 36 - 37. All the English translations in this book are my own.

11. Antonio Papell, *Moratín y su época* (Palma de Mallorca: Atlante, 1958), p. 101. Jiménez Salas also names these participants in the *tertulia*,

with the exception of Luis Godoy, pp. 78 - 79. See also John Dowling, *Leandro Fernández de Moratín* (New York: Twayne Publishers, Inc., 1971), pp. 21 - 23.

12. Quoted by Leopoldo Augusto de Cueto, "Bosquejo histórico-crítico de la poesía castellana en el siglo XVIII," *Biblioteca de Autores Españoles* (hereinafter cited as *BAE*), 61 (Madrid: Rivadeneyra, 1869), note to p. cxlvi.

13. The poem is published in Jiménez Salas, p. 80.

Chapter Two

1. Juan Pablo Forner, *Cotejo de las églogas que ha premiado la Real Academia de la Lengua,* ed. Fernando Lázaro (Salamanca: Consejo Superior de Investigaciones Científicas, 1951), p. 27.

2. *Ibid.,* p. 48.

3. "Gothicism" was a term used by the eighteenth-century writers to refer to those who seemed to be living — and thinking — in the Middle Ages.

4. [Tomás de Iriarte], *Para casos tales suelen tener los maestros oficiales: epístola crítico-parenética o exhortación patética que escribió D. Eleuterio Geta al autor de las "Fábulas literarias" en vista del papel intitulado "El asno erudito"* (Madrid: Imprenta de Andrés de Sotos, 1782), p. 21.

5. R. Merritt Cox, *Tomás de Iriarte* (New York: Twayne Publishers, 1972), pp. 42 - 45.

6. Cotarelo, *Iriarte y su época,* p. 257n. All the documents by Iriarte and Forner related to this episode, as well as the responses of the authorities, are reprinted in the appendix to Polt's edition of *Los gramáticos,* pp. 229 - 56.

7. José Jurado, "Repercusiones del pleito con Iriarte en la obra literaria de Forner," *Thesaurus: Boletín del Instituto Caro y Cuervo,* 24 (1969), 234n. The sonnet — "Lamiendo reconoce al beneficio" — is published in *BAE,* 63 (1871), 54.

Chapter Three

1. [Nicolás] Masson de Morvilliers, "Espagne," in *Encyclopédie méthodique, Géographie,* I (Paris: Panckoucke, 1783), 566.

2. *Ibid.,* p. 561.

3. *Ibid.,* p. 566.

4. *Ibid.,* p. 565.

5. See the discussion of the French critics of Spain in A. Zamora Vicente's edition of the *Oración apologética por la España y su mérito literario* (Badajoz: Imprenta de la Excelentísima Diputación, 1945), pp. x - xi.

6. Cited by Cotarelo, pp. 297 - 98.

7. The sonnet is reprinted in Cotarelo, pp. 294 - 95, from Iriarte's *Obras en verso y prosa,* VII (Madrid: Imprenta Real, 1805), 344.

8. Cited by Cotarelo, p. 295; and by Jurado, pp. 253 - 54, with minor variants. The title of the sonnet appears only in Jurado.

9. *Carta de Don Juan Pablo Forner, abogado de los Reales Consejos, a Don Ignacio López de Ayala, catedrático de poesía en el Colegio de San Isidro de esta corte; sobre haberle desaprobado su drama intitulado "La cautiva española,"* in *BAE*, 63 (1871), 375.

10. *Ibid.*, pp. 377 - 78.

11. Juan Sempere y Guarinos, *Ensayo de una biblioteca española de los mejores escritores del reynado de Carlos III*, I (Madrid: Imprenta Real, 1785), 40 - 41.

12. Cited by Jiménez Salas, p. 96.

13. *Ibid.*

14. *Ibid.*, p. 97.

15. *Oración apologética*, p. 5.

16. *Ibid.*, pp. 5 - 6. There are several versions of this story in the critical works about Forner. Zamora Vicente, in the introductory study to his edition of the *Oración apologética* (p. xxiv), simply says that Forner published it in French because that was the language understood by everyone. Francisco Fernández González, in his *Historia de la crítica literaria en España desde Luzán hasta nuestros días* (Madrid: Imprenta de D. Alejandro Gómez Fuentenebro, 1867), follows Forner's story about the "illustrious gentleman" but says that it was Pedro Rodríguez de Campomanes (p. 40). Jiménez Salas remains the authority, by quoting Floridablanca's letter (p. 97). She does not, however, point out the inconsistency of the documents and Forner's questionable version of the publication details.

17. *Oración apologética*, p. 6.

18. *Ibid.*, p. 12.

19. Vicente García de la Huerta, *Theatro Hespañol*, I (Madrid: Imprenta Real, 1785), p. 3 of the dedicatory, without pagination.

20. Cotarelo, pp. 334 - 35.

21. Huerta, *Theatro Hespañol*, I, ccv.

22. [Félix María de Samaniego], *Continuación de las memorias críticas de Cosme Damián*, in *Obras inéditas o poco conocidas del insigne fabulista D. Félix María de Samaniego*, ed. Estaquio Fernández de Navarrete (Vitoria: Hijos de Manteli, 1866), p. 136. Samaniego's choice of a pseudonym has never been explained, as far as I know. A possible explanation is in a curious note in the *Diario de Madrid* (June 20, 1794) which announces a rummage sale "on St. Isabel Street, in the house on the corner of St. Cosme and St. Damián, no. 7, where the ambassador from France lived." If the French ambassador lived in that same house in 1785, the pseudonym could be a reference to Huerta's discussion of the "transpyrenaics."

23. Samaniego, *Obras inéditas*, p. 135.

24. *Ibid.*, p. 147. For information about the dramatists who rewrote the seventeenth-century plays, see Navarrete's note 16 in the *Obras inéditas*, pp.

138 - 39, and John A. Cook, *Neo-Classic Drama in Spain: Theory and Practice* (Dallas: Southern Methodist University Press, 1959), pp. 260 - 70.

25. Vicente García de la Huerta, *Lección crítica a los lectores del papel intitulado "Continuación de las memorias críticas de Cosme Damián"* (Madrid: Imprenta Real, 1785), p. xxvi.

26. *Ibid.*, note to p. xliii.

27. Juan Pablo Forner, *Reflexiones sobre la "Lección crítica" que ha publicado Don Vicente García de la Huerta: las escribía en vindicación de la buena memoria de Miguel de Cervantes Saavedra Tomé Cecial, ex-excudero del bachiller Sansón Carrasco* (Madrid: Imprenta Real, 1786), p. 52.

28. *Ibid.*, pp. 117 - 20.

29. *Ibid.*, p. 85.

30. *Ibid.*, p. 116n.

31. *Ibid.*, p. 142.

32. Vicente García de la Huerta, *La Escena Hespañola defendida en el "Prólogo" del "Theatro Hespañol" de D. Vicente García de la Huerta y en su "Lección crítica"* (Madrid: Hilario Santos, 1786), first page of the prologue to the reprinted prologue, no pagination.

33. *Ibid.*, note to p. XXVI.

34. *Ibid.*, note to p. XLVIII.

35. *Ibid.*, note to pp. XCVII - VIII.

36. *Ibid.*, note to p. CIV [*sic* for CLIV].

37. *Fe de erratas del "Prólogo" del "Theatro Hespañol"* in *BAE*, 63 (1871), 343.

38. Cited by Jiménez Salas, p. 417.

39. Cited by Cotarelo, p. 341.

40. *BAE*, 63 (1871), 343.

41. Cited by Cotarelo, p. 344.

42. Josef Conchudo [pseud.?], *Carta al autor de la "Oración apologética por la España y su mérito literario"* (Madrid: Manuel González, 1787), p. 3.

43. *Ibid.*, p. 21.

44. *Ibid.*, p. 4.

45. *Correo de Madrid*, I (1787), 368.

46. Cotarelo, p. 318.

47. Jiménez Salas, p. 418.

48. [Juan Pablo Forner], *Conversaciones familiares entre "El Censor," "El Apologista Universal," y un doctor en leyes: en las cuales se procura hacer el panegírico de aquellos dos grandes maestros de nuestra nación, y se da a conocer el mérito de sus inmortales escritos. Publica la primera y continuará en publicar otras muchas Don Silvio Liberio, que se pone a escritor periódico, porque no sabe ponerse a otra cosa* (Madrid: n.p., 1787), p. 22. Cited by Cotarelo, p. 318.

49. The full title is *Demostraciones palmarias de que "El Censor," su "Corresponsal," "El Apologista Universal," y los demás papelejos de este jaez no sirven de nada al estado ni a la literatura de España. Las escribe el*

bachiller Regañadientes para ver si quiere Dios que nos libremos de una vez de esta plaga de críticos y discursistas menudos que nos aturden (Clear Demonstrations That "The Censor," its "Correspondent," "The Universal Apologist," and the Other Fat Papers of This Ilk Serve For Nothing to the State Nor to the Literature of Spain. Written by the Graduate Tooth-Gnasher In Order to See If God Wants Us to Free Ourselves Once and For All From This Plague of Minute Critics and Discursists That Assail Us) (Madrid: n.p., 1787).

50. Cotarelo, p. 320.

51. *Antisofisma, o sea, desenredo de los sofismas con que se ha pretendido obscurecer algunas doctrinas de la "Oración apologética por la España y su mérito literario" de D. Juan Pablo Forner, por E. C. V.* (Madrid: Blas Román, 1787), p. xxxiii.

52. *Ibid.*, pp. lv - lvi.

53. *Ibid.*, p. xxxi.

54. Cotarelo, p. 321. There is a detailed resumé of Borrego's *Historia universal* and of Forner's critique in Joaquín María Sotelo, "Elogio del señor Don Juan Pablo Forner," *BAE*, 63 (1871), 282 - 83.

55. Anon. [Antonio Borrego ? Iriarte?], *Cartas de un español residente en París a su hermano residente en Madrid sobre la "Oración apologética por la España y su mérito literario," de D. Juan Pablo Forner* (Madrid: Imprenta Real, 1788), p. 113. Cited by Cotarelo, pp. 321 - 22.

56. Cotarelo, p. 322.

Chapter Four

1. Cited by Cueto, p. cxxvi.

2. *Las majas: poema chusqui-heroico por D. Melchor María Sánchez Toledano* (Madrid: D. Antonio Espinosa, 1789), canto III.

3. "Representación de Forner a Floridablanca, 1 de junio de 1783," in the appendix to Polt's edition of *Los gramáticos*, p. 240.

4. Jiménez Salas, p. 371.

5. Eugenio Habela Patiño [pseud.?], *Apéndice a la primera salida de Don Quixote el escolástico* (Madrid: Antonio Espinosa, 1789), p. 56.

6. Sempere, *Ensayo de una biblioteca*, VI (1789), 61 - 62.

7. *Ibid.*, pp. 91 - 92.

8. *Ibid.*, p. 95.

9. *Ibid.*, pp. 107 - 08.

10. *Ibid.*, p. 190.

11. *Ibid.*, pp. 216 - 17.

12. In volume III of the *Ensayo de una biblioteca* (1786) the Forner article is on pages 84 - 94, the additional note on page 218.

13. *Ibid.*, p. 104.

14. *Ibid.*, p. 116.

15. *Ibid.*, pp. 117 - 18.

16. Juan Pablo Forner, *Suplemento al artículo "Trigueros" comprehendido en el tomo 6° del "Ensayo de una biblioteca de los mejores escritores del reynado de Carlos III," por el Dr. D. Juan Sempere y Guarinos* (Salamanca: Don Francisco de Toxar, 1790), p. 11.

17. *Ibid.*, p. 62.

18. *Ibid.*, p. 57.

19. Cotarelo, pp. 379 - 80.

20. Forner, *Suplemento*, pp. 57 - 58.

21. *Ibid.*, p. 61.

22. *Ibid.*, p. 63.

23. *Ibid.*, p. 65.

24. Cited by Cotarelo, p. 382.

25. Cited by Cueto, p. cxxv.

26. Papell, *Moratín y su época*, p. 63.

27. [Tomás Antonio Sánchez], *Carta de Paracuellos, escrita por D. Fernando Pérez a un sobrino que se hallaba en peligro de ser autor de un libro* (Madrid: Viuda de Ibarra, 1789), p. 70n.

28. *Ibid.*, p. 92n.

29. *Ibid.*, p. 65.

30. [Juan Pablo Forner], *Carta de Bartolo el sobrino de Don Fernando Pérez, tercianario de Paracuellos, al editor de la carta de su tío* (Madrid: Imprenta Real, 1790), pp. 44n - 45n.

31. *Ibid.*, pp. 57 - 58.

32. Sempere, *Ensayo de una biblioteca*, V (1789), 6 - 7.

33. *Ibid.*, p. 5.

34. *Ibid.*, pp. 8 - 9.

35. *Ibid.*, p. 9.

36. [Tomás Antonio Sánchez], *Defensa de D. Fernando Pérez, autor de la "Carta de Paracuellos," impugnado por el licenciado Paulo Ipnocausto* (Madrid: Viuda de Ibarra, 1790), p. 9.

37. *Ibid.*, p. 35.

38. Forner, *Exequias*, p. 6.

Chapter Five

1. Jiménez Salas, p. 108.

2. Jiménez Salas only finds documentation for the first two children. Villanueva mentions all three in the "Noticia bibliográfica" in *BAE*, 63 (1871), 266. Sotelo's "Elogio" provides the information about the academy honors in Seville (*BAE*, 63 [1871], 288n and 289). In "Forner y Blanco: dos vertientes del XVIII" *Cuadernos americanos*, 148, no. 5 (septiembre-octubre 1966), pp. 128 - 38, Iris M. Zavala provides interesting data about a verse letter from Blanco to Forner criticizing the *Philosophical Discourses*. The letter, reprinted by Zavala from *BAE*, 62 (1870), 661 - 62, was written in 1796. Zavala erroneously states that Forner wrote the *Discourses* in 1787, the

year in which they were published, seven years after their composition.

3. The letter was first published by Villanueva in the *Seminario pintoresco español*, 9 (1844), 167 - 68. It is reprinted in *BAE*, 62 (1870), 213.

4. Cited by Jiménez Salas, p. 120.

5. *Ibid.*

6. *Ibid.*, p. 121.

7. *Ibid.*, p. 123.

8. [Juan Pablo Forner], *La corneja sin plumas: fragmento póstumo del licenciado Paulo Ipnocausto* (Puerto de Santa María: Don Luis de Luque y Leyva, 1795), p. 5.

9. *Ibid.*, pp. 48 - 49.

10. *Ibid.*, p. 6.

11. *Ibid.*, p. 67.

12. See Cotarelo, pp. 394n - 95n for a list of these works, which I have also included below in the bibliography of works by Forner.

13. See Estala's letter to Forner, *BAE*, 61 (1869), note to p. cxliv.

14. *Correo de Madrid*, VII (1790), 196.

15. *Ibid.*, p. 200.

16. Cited by Cotarelo, p. 398n.

17. *BAE*, 61 (1869), note to p. cxliv.

18. "Apología del vulgo con relación a la poesía dramática," in *La escuela de la amistad, o el filósofo enamorado* (Madrid: Fermín Villalpando, 1796), p. xvi.

19. Jiménez Salas, p. 40.

20. Sotelo, p. 297.

Chapter Six

1. Juan Pablo Forner, *Carta del tonto de la duquesa de Alba a un amigo suyo de América*, in *BAE*, 63 (1871), 345.

2. Cited from [Charles] Nodier by Antonio Rubio in *La crítica del galicismo en España (1726 - 1832)* (Mexico: Universidad Nacional de México, 1937), p. 90.

3. Forner, *Exequias*, p. 25.

4. *Ibid.*, p. 135.

5. Sempere, *Ensayo de una biblioteca*, III, 128 - 29.

6. *Ibid.*, II, 31.

7. *Exequias*, p. 115.

8. *Ibid.*, p. 186. For information on *La Espigadera*, see Cook, *Neo-Classic Drama in Spain*, pp. 325 - 28.

9. [Forner], *La corneja sin plumas*, pp. 3 - 4.

10. [Juan Pablo Forner], *El asno erudito* (Madrid: Imprenta del Supremo Consejo de Indias, 1782), p. 3 and p.10.

11. [Sánchez], *Carta de Paracuellos*, p. i.

12. *Ibid.*, p. iv.

13. [Sánchez], *Defensa de D. Fernando Pérez*, pp. 29 - 30. In the quotation, Sánchez is mocking Forner's use of the archaic *senda* to mean *scant*, and *luenga*, an archaic form meaning *long*. The "nose" quotation is the first line of a famous sonnet by Quevedo: "*Erase un hombre a un nariz pegado.*"

14. [Forner], *Carta de Bartolo*, pp. 78 - 79.

15. Forner, *Reflexiones . . . [de] Tomé Cecial*, p. 6.

16. *Ibid.*, p. 18.

17. *Ibid.*, p. 82.

18. *Ibid.*, pp. 66 - 67.

19. Forner, *Suplemento*, p. 17.

20. *Ibid.*, p. 49n.

21. *Ibid.*, p. 59.

22. Forner, *Los gramáticos*, p. 190.

23. *Ibid.* "Thrasonic" and "Pyrgopolynicitic" are references to two pompous characters in Roman drama: Thraso in Terence's *The Eunuch* and Pyrgopolynices in Plautus' *Miles gloriosus* (see Polt's note to page 148, *Los gramáticos*).

24. *Ibid.*, pp. 196 - 97.

Chapter Seven

1. Forner, *Exequias*, p. 179. The italics are mine.

2. Forner, *Cotejo de las églogas*, p. 6.

3. *Exequias*, p. 45.

4. *Ibid.*, pp. 125 - 26.

5. *Ibid.*, p. 57.

6. *Ibid.*, p. 104.

7. *Ibid.*, p. 87.

8. [Iriarte], *Para casos tales*, p. 3.

9. *Ibid.*, p. 19.

10. *Ibid.*, p. 54.

11. *Ibid.*, p. 27.

12. *Ibid.*, p. 30.

13. Forner, *Los gramáticos*, p. 82.

14. *Ibid.*, pp. 83 - 84.

15. Forner, *Reflexiones . . . [de] Tomé Cecial*, p. 6.

16. *Exequias*, p. 57.

17. *Cotejo de las églogas*, p. 10.

18. *Exequias*, p. 82.

19. *Los gramáticos*, p. 59.

20. *Ibid.*, p. 87.

21. *Ibid.*, p. 59.

22. "Causas del mal gusto en la poesía," in *Obras de Don Juan Pablo*

Forner, ed. Luis Villanueva (Madrid: Imprenta de la Amistad, 1844), pp. 147 - 48.

23. *Exequias*, p. 80.

24. *Reflexiones . . . [de] Tomé Cecial*, p. 53.

25. *Ibid.*, pp. 95n - 96n.

Chapter Eight

1. Forner, *Exequias*, pp. 44 - 45.

2. *Ibid.*, pp. 91 - 92.

3. *Ibid.*, pp. 93 - 94.

4. *Ibid.*, pp. 111 - 12.

5. *Ibid.*, pp. 144 - 45.

6. *Ibid.*, p. 172.

7. Forner, *Oración apologética*, pp. 9 - 14.

8. Masson never says exactly that, though he always implies it with statements like: "What can you expect from a people who look to a monk for permission to read and think?" (*Encyclopédie Méthodique, Géographie*, I: 565).

9. *Oración apologética*, pp. 28 - 29.

10. *Ibid.*, pp. 69 - 80. The asterisks indicate the divisions between the marginal notes.

11. *Ibid.*, p. 29.

12. *Ibid.*, p. 32.

13. *Ibid.*, pp. 123 - 24.

14. *Ibid.*, pp. 34 - 35.

15. Forner, *Antisofisma*, pp. xxiv - vi.

16. Juan Pablo Forner, *Preservativo contra el ateismo* (Sevilla: D. Félix de la Puerta, 1795), pp. i - iv.

17. Forner, *Obras*, pp. 201 - 202.

18. *Ibid.*, p. 210.

19. *Ibid.*, p. 214.

20. *Ibid.*, p. 228.

21. *Ibid.*, p. 231.

22. *Oración apologética*, p. 8.

Chapter Nine

1. Cueto, p. cxliv.

2. Cotarelo, *Iriarte y su época*, p. 361.

3. The play is published in *Teatro nuevo español*, I (Madrid: B. García y compañía, 1800), 197 - 339.

4. Forner, *Exequias*, pp. 115 - 16.

5. *Ibid.*, p. 119.

6. Forner, "Apología del vulgo," pp. v - vi.
7. Forner, *Carta . . . a don Ignacio López de Ayala*, p. 376.
8. Forner, *Reflexiones . . . [de] Tomé Cecial*, p. 25.
9. *Ibid.*, p. 42.
10. *Correo de Madrid*, VII (1790), 198.
11. *BAE*, 63 (1871), 377.
12. *Ibid.*
13. *Ibid.*
14. *Ibid.*, p. 375.
15. *Ibid.*, p. 377.
16. *Ibid.*, pp. 375 - 76.
17. Forner, *La escuela de la amistad, o el filósofo enamorado*, p. 4.
18. *Ibid.*, p. 9.
19. *Ibid.*, p. 21.
20. *Ibid.*, p. 34.
21. Forner, "Apología del vulgo," p. xxxi.
22. *Ibid.*, p. xxxvii.

Chapter Ten

1. Forner, *Exequias*, pp. 61 - 62.
2. *Ibid.*, p. 75.
3. *Ibid.*, p. 76.
4. *Ibid.*, pp. 144 - 45.
5. *Ibid.*, p. 162.
6. *Ibid.*, p. 55.
7. *Ibid.*, pp. 55 - 56.
8. *Ibid.*, pp. 65 - 66.
9. *Ibid.*, pp. 155 - 56.
10. [Forner], *La corneja sin plumas*, p. 37.
11. *Ibid.*, pp. 41 - 44.
12. *Ibid.*, p. 38.
13. *Ibid.*, pp. 38 - 41.
14. *Ibid.*, pp. 66 - 67.

Selected Bibliography

PRIMARY SOURCES

Many of the works by Forner and the writers who engaged in polemics with him are very difficult to find today. The most extensive collections in the United States are in the George Ticknor Collection of the Boston Public Library and in the Hispanic Society of America in New York City. There are complete catalogues available for each of these collections. The Library of Congress catalogue provides information about the location of some of these works in university libraries.

Because almost everything that Forner wrote was a response to something else, I have listed first the works of Forner and then the other writers' works that either occasioned Forner's works or responded to them. I have arranged the works in alphabetical order, with the probable date of composition in brackets, if it differs from the date of publication. The items are numbered to facilitate my indications of the relationship between the different works.

I.   Works by Forner

1.   *Obras de Don Juan Pablo Forner*, ed. Luis Villanueva (Madrid: Impren-ta de la Amistad, 1844). The first volume of a projected complete works. No more were published. Contains discourses, treatises, and some poetry, but none of the important works.
2.   *Forner*, ed. N. González Ruiz (Madrid: Editora Nacional, 1941). One of the series "Breviarios del Pensamiento Español." This collection of short quotations from Forner's work is precisely the sort of thing that Forner satirized in the *Exquias de la lengua castellana*. Of little use other than as an introduction to his ideology.
3.   *Poesías*, ed. Leopoldo Augusto de Cueto, in *Poetas líricos del siglo XVIII*, volume II, *Biblioteca de Autores Españoles* (hereinafter cited as *BAE*), 63 (Madrid: Rivadeneyra, 1871), 297 - 374.

147

4. *Antisofisma, o sea, desenredo de los sofismas con que se ha pretendido obscurecer algunas doctrinas de la "Oración apologética por la España y su mérito literario" de D. Juan Pablo Forner, por E. C. V.* (Madrid: Blas Román, 1787). Reply to Conchudo, item 39.

5. *El asno erudito. Fábula original. Obra póstuma de un poeta anónimo. Publícala D. Pablo Segarra* (Madrid: Imprenta del Supremo Consejo de Indias, 1782). Attack on Iriarte, item 46. The copy of this rare first edition in the University of Wisconsin library is bound with a manuscript of Samaniego's *Observaciones sobre las Fábulas literarias originales de Don Tomás de Iriarte*, published anonymously in 1782. The Iriartes were trying to find out who wrote the *Observaciones* when they found the *Grammarians* manuscript. Forner's fable, without his introduction, is reprinted in Cotarelo, *Iriarte y su época*, pp. 540 - 44.

    El asno erudito, ed. M. Muñoz Cortes (Valencia: Castalia, 1948). An edition with introduction and notes.

6. *Carta de Bartolo el sobrino de Don Fernando Pérez, tercianario de Paracuellos, al editor de la carta de su tío. Publícala el licenciado Paulo Ipnocausto* (Madrid: Imprenta Real, 1790). Reply to Sánchez, item 54.

7. *Carta de Don Antonio Varas al autor de "La riada" sobre la composición de este poema* (Madrid: Don Miguel Escribano, 1784). Criticism of Trigueros, item 57.

8. *Carta de Don Juan Pablo Forner, abogado de los Reales Consejos, a Don Ignacio López de Ayala, catedrático de poesía en el Colegio de San Isidro de esta corte; sobre haberle desaprobado su drama intitulado "La cautiva española."* [1784] Unpublished at the time, but included in *BAE*, 63 (Madrid, 1871), 374 - 78.

9. *Carta del Diario de Madrid de 28 de abril impugnando la comedia del "Filósofo enamorado" a la que sigue una defensa de la expresada crítica por un amigo del autor de la comedia* (Cadiz: Manuel Ximénez Carreño, n.d. [1796]). Forner's defense of his play, item 20.

10. *Carta del tonto de la duquesa de Alba a un amigo suyo de América* [1783]. Unpublished during Forner's lifetime, included in *BAE*, 63 (Madrid, 1871), 345 - 48.

11. *Carta dirigida a un vecino de Cádiz sobre otra del L. J. A. C., un literato sevillano, con el título de "La loa restituida a su primitivo ser." Su autor Rosauro de Safo. Con una epístola de Leandro Misono en nombre del literato sevillano* (Cádiz: Don Manuel Ximénez Carreño, n.d. [1796]). Reply to Alvarez Caballero, item 36. Reprinted in Cotarelo, *Bibliografía de las controversias*, pp. 277 - 81.

12. *Continuación a la carta del autor de la comedia del "Filósofo enamorado" publicada en el Diario de Cádiz de 13 de mayo pasado de este año en respuesta a la de D. Hugo Imparcial, que también se publicó en el Diario de 28 de abril* (Cádiz: Antonio Murguia, 1796). Continuation of item 9.

13. *Consulta que Don Juan Pablo Forner como fiscal que era de la Audien-*

cia de Sevilla hizo al Consejo de Castilla sobre que debían representarse comedias en la ciudad del Puerto de Santa María, sin embargo de haberse opuesto a ello la real Audiencia y el Acuerdo [1795?] (Madrid: Imprenta de Burgos, 1816). Interesting manifestation of the Seville theater dispute, in which Forner defends the theater as beneficial to the public and attacks the "tasteless" public spectacle of the bullfight.

14. *Conversaciones familiares entre "El Censor," "El Apologista Universal," y un doctor en leyes: en las cuales se procura hacer el panegírico de aquellos dos grandes maestros de nuestra nación, y se da a conocer el mérito de sus inmortales escritos. Publica la primera y continuará en publicar otras muchas Don Silvio Liberio, que se pone a escritor periódico porque no sabe ponerse a otra cosa* (Madrid: n. p., 1787). One of the responses to the critics of the *Oración apologética*, item 26.

15. *La corneja sin plumas: fragmento póstumo del licenciado Paulo Ipnocausto* (Puerto de Santa María: Don Luis de Luque y Leyva, 1795). Attack on Vargas y Ponce, item 58.

16. *Cotejo de las églogas que ha premiado la Real Academia de la Lengua* ed. Fernando Lázaro [1781] (Salamanca: Consejo Superior de Investigaciones Científicas, 1951). Response to Iriarte, item 49, in defense of Meléndez Valdés, item 51.

17. *Demostraciones palmarias de que "El Censor," su "Corresponsal," "El Apologista Universal," y los demás papelejos de este jaez no sirven de nada al estado ni a la literatura de España. Las escribe el bachiller Regañadientes para ver si quiere Dios que nos libremos de una vez de esta plaga de críticos y discursistas menudos que nos aturden* (Madrid: n. p., 1787). Response to journalistic attacks on the *Oración apologética*, item 26.

18. *Diálogo entre D. Silvestre, D. Crisóstomo y D. Plácido. Precédelo un prólogo al público sevillano* [1796?]. Defense of the theater from the charge that it corrupts the morals of the masses. Part of the Seville dispute. The text of this manuscript was published for the first time in Cotarelo, *Bibliografía de las controversias*, pp. 293 - 319.

19. *Discursos filosóficos sobre el hombre* [1780?] (Madrid: Imprenta Real, 1787). The *Discursos*, without the extensive notes in prose, are reprinted in *BAE*, 63 (Madrid, 1871), 354 - 74. Responses to the *Discursos* include Fox Novel, item 41; Habela Patiño, item 42; and Trigueros, item 56.

20. *La escuela de la amistad, o el filósofo enamorado* [1790] (Madrid: Fermín Villalpando, 1796). This edition has the preface, "Apología del vulgo con relación a la poesía dramática." I have seen three other pamphlet editions of this play, all without the preface (Valencia: J. de Orga, 1796; Barcelona: En la oficina de Pablo Nadal, 1797; and Barcelona: Juan Francisco Piferrer, n. d.). See ESTALA in the secondary bibliography below for letters related to this play, and items 9 and 12 for Forner's defenses of his play.

21. *Exequias de la lengua castellana* [1788?], ed. Pedro Sáinz y Rodríguez

(Madrid: Espasa-Calpe, 1956). This is number 66 of the Clásicos Castellanos collection, a reprint of the 1925 edition in that series. The work was first published in the *BAE*, volume 63, in 1871 and again in 1917, pp. 378 - 425. The "Reflexiones sobre el teatro en España" (pp. 115 - 21) was first published unsigned in the journal *La Espigadera* in 1790 (see Cook, *Neo-Classic Drama in Spain*, pp. 325 - 28 and pp. 384 - 92).

22. "La farsa de los filósofos," in the *Diario de las musas*, December 7, 1790, pp. 27 - 29, and December 10, 1790, pp. 43 - 45. This article is un-signed, but Forner claims it as his in the list of works reprinted in Villanueva, item 1, pp. xxiii - xxiv.

23. *Fe de erratas del "Prólogo" del "Theatro Hespañol" de Don Vicente García de la Huerta* [1786]. Unpublished at the time. Fragments are published in *BAE*, 63 (Madrid, 1871), 269 - 70. Reply to Huerta, items 43 and 45.

24. *Los gramáticos: historia chinesca* [1782], ed. John H. R. Polt (Berkeley: University of California Press, 1970). Volume 95 of the University of California Publications in Modern Philology. Attack on Iriarte, in response to item 48.

  Los gramáticos: historia chinesca, ed. José Jurado (Madrid: Espasa-Calpe, 1970). This edition, like Polt's, contains in an appendix many documents related to the *Gramáticos* affair.

25. *Introducción a la loa que se recitó para la apertura del teatro en Sevilla, año de 1795, con una carta que sirve de prólogo, escrita por un literato no sevillano a un amigo suyo de Cádiz* (Cádiz: D. Antonio Murguia, 1796). The work that started the polemic over the theater in Seville which led to items 11, 13, 18, 32, 33, and 36.

26. *Oración apologética por la España y su mérito literario, para que sirva de exornación al "Discurso" leído por el Abate Denina en la Academia de Ciencias de Berlin respondiendo a la cuestión "¿Qué se debe a España?"* [1785?] (Madrid: Imprenta Real, 1786). This reply to Masson (item 50) includes Denina's address in French (item 40) and the "Contestación al Discurso CXIII del *Censor*."

  Oración apologética por la España y su mérito literario, ed. A. Zamora Vicente (Badajoz: Imprenta de la Excelentísima Diputación, 1945). An edition of Forner's preface, the *Oración* and Forner's notes, without the Denina address or the reply to *The Censor*. An introduction by Zamora.

  Oración apologética por la España y su mérito literario (Madrid: Ibarra, 1956). An edition of Denina's address in Spanish and the *Oración*, but without Forner's notes and preface, and without the reply to *The Censor*.

27. *Pasatiempo de D. Juan Pablo Forner en respuesta a las objeciones que se han hecho a su "Oración apologética por la España"* (Madrid: Im-

prenta Real, 1787). Answer to journalistic attacks on the *Oración*.

28. *La paz: canto heroyco* (Madrid: Villalpando, 1796). Dedicated to Godoy, the Prince of the Peace. Includes a preface, "Razón de este poema."

29. *Preservativo contra el ateísmo* (Sevilla: D. Félix de la Puerta, 1795).

30. *Reflexiones sobre el modo de escribir la historia de España* (Madrid: Imprenta de Burgos, 1816). A curious edition, which is a condensation of the *Discursos sobre el modo de escribir y mejorar la historia de España*, in Villanueva, item 1. In a note (p. 1), Villanueva accuses the poet Antonio Valladares of having stolen and mutilated Forner's work. Even Forner's preface is rewritten.

31. *Reflexiones sobre la "Lección crítica" que ha publicado Don Vicente García de la Huerta: las escribía en vindicación de la buena memoria de Miguel de Cervantes Saavedra Tomé Cecial, ex-excudero del bachiller Sansón Carrasco. Las publica D. Juan Pablo Forner* (Madrid: Imprenta Real, 1786). Reply to Huerta, items 44 and 45. Huerta's response is item 43.

32. *Respuesta a los "Desengaños útiles y avisos importantes del literato de Ecija"* [1796?]. A reply to another attack on Forner's ideas about theater during the Seville dispute. Published for the first time in Cotarelo, *Bibliografía de las controversias*, pp. 381 - 93.

33. *Respuesta del cura de Mairenilla la Taconera a la carta de Juan Perote, sacristán de Armencilla. Su fecha en Cádiz a 19 de marzo de 1796. Publicada en la misma ciudad a 23 de mayo del propio año* (Cádiz: D. Antonio Murguia, 1796). Part of the theater dispute in Seville. Reprinted in Cotarelo, *Bibliografía de las controversias*, pp. 271 - 77.

34. *Sátira contra los vicios introducidos en la poesía castellana, premiada por la Real Academia Española en junta que celebró el día 15 de octubre de 1782* (Madrid: Don Joaquín Ibarra, 1782). The *Sátira* is reprinted in Villanueva (item 1), pp. 149 - 74, and in *BAE*, 63 (Madrid, 1871), 304 - 10.

35. *Suplemento al artículo "Trigueros" comprehendido en el tomo 6° del "Ensayo de una biblioteca de los mejores escritores del reynado de Carlos III," por el Dr. D. Juan Sempere y Guarinos* (Salamanca: Don Francisco de Toxar, 1790). Reply to the Trigueros article in Sempere, item 55.

II. Works by Forner's Contemporaries

36. ALVAREZ CABALLERO, JOSÉ. *La loa restituida a su primitivo ser: carta de un literato sevillano a un amigo suyo de otro pueblo, en que se demuestra el verdadero espíritu de la loa que sirivó para la apertura del teatro en esta ciudad contra las interpretaciones del literato no sevillano. Se impugna solidamente el teatro y se descubren los errores que en su*

152 JUAN PABLO FORNER

vindicación ha esparcido el apologista (Sevilla: Imprenta de los Señores Hijos de Hidalgo y González de la Bonilla, 1796). Response to Forner, item 25. Forner's counterreply is item 11.

37. ANON.[Antonio Borrego? Iriarte?]. *Cartas de un español residente en París a su hermano residente en Madrid sobre la "Oración apologética por la España y su mérito literario," de D. Juan Pablo Forner* (Madrid: Imprenta Real, 1788). Forner's response was the *Lista puntual de errores*, which has never been published.

38. CAVANILLES, ANTONIO JOSÉ DE. *Observations de M. l'abbé Cavanilles sur l'article "Espagne" de la Nouvelle Encyclopédie* (Paris: Alex. Jombart, 1784). Answer to Masson, item 50.

Observaciones sobre el artículo "España" de la Nueva Encyclopedia escritas en francés por el doctor D. Antonio Cabanilles [sic], *presbítero, y traducidas al castellano por Don Mariano Rivera* (Madrid: Imprenta Real, 1784). The translator indicates in his preface that he has omitted some of the notes from the French edition, notes very much to the point in France, but superfluous in an edition for Spaniards.

39. CONCHUDO, JOSEF [pseud.?]. *Carta al autor de la "Oración apologética por la España y su mérito literario"* (Madrid: Manuel González, 1787). Response to Forner, item 26. Forner's reply was the *Antisofisma*, item 4.

40. DENINA, CARLO. "Résponse à la question: 'Que doit-on à l'Espagne?' Discours à l'Academie de Berlin dans l'assemblée publique du 26 Janvier l'an 1786 pour le jour anniversaire du Roi, par l'abbé Denina." Appeared in French in Forner's *Oración* (Madrid, 1786), and was published in Spanish in the 1956 edition of the same, item 26. The "Discours" is an answer to Masson, item 50.

41. FOX NOVEL, M. [pseud.? Iriarte?]. *Centones fornerianos: discurso antisofístico extractado del "Hombre" de Forner y traducido al quákaro* (Madrid: En Casa de González, 1788). An attack on Forner's *Discursos filosóficos*, item 19.

42. HABELA PATIÑO, EUGENIO [pseud.?]. *Apéndice a la primera salida de Don Quixote el escolástico* (Madrid: Antonio Espinosa, 1789). An attack on Roselli's *Philosophical Compendium* and on Forner's *Discursos*, item 19.

43. HUERTA, VICENTE GARCÍA DE LA. *La Escena Hespañola defendida en el "Prólogo" del "Theatro Hespañol" de D. Vicente García de la Huerta y en su "Lección crítica"* (Madrid: Hilario Santos, 1786). This is a reprint of the prologue to volume I of the *Theatro Hespañol*, item 45, in response to Forner, item 31. Huerta adds notes to the prologue intensifyng his attack on Cervantes and on Forner.

44. ———. *Lección crítica a los lectores del papel intitulado "Continuación de las memorias críticas de Cosme Damián"* (Madrid: Imprenta Real, 1785).Reply to Samaniego, item 52. Here Huerta makes the *tuerto* com-

ment about Forner in response to item 8. Forner's reply is item 31.

45. ———. *Theatro Hespañol.* 17 vols. (Madrid: Imprenta Real, 1785 - 86). The prologue to volume I drew the attacks, to which Huerta responded with items 44 and 43.

46. IRIARTE, TOMÁS DE. *Fábulas literarias en verso castellano: dalas a luz un amigo del autor* (Madrid: Imprenta Real, 1782). The work that inspired Forner's *El asno erudito*, item 5.

47. ———. *La felicidad de la vida del campo: égloga impresa por la Real Academia Española por ser, entre todas las presentadas, la que más se acerca a la que ganó el premio. Su autor, Don Francisco Agustín de Cisneros* (Madrid: Joaquín Ibarra, 1780). The poem that lost to Meléndez' eclogue, item 51.

48. ———. *Para casos tales suelen tener los maestros oficiales: epístola crítico-parenética o exhortación patética que escribió D. Eleuterio Geta al autor de las "Fábulas literarias" en vista del papel intitulado "El asno erudito"* (Madrid: Imprenta de Andrés de Sotos, 1782). Response to Forner, item 5.

49. ———. *Reflexiones sobre la égloga intitulada "Batilo," compuesta en alabanza de la vida del campo por Don Juan Meléndez Valdés* [1782]. Iriarte's reaction to the Academy's decision in favor of Meléndez, item 51. Forner replied with the *Cotejo*, item 16. I have found no reference to an edition of Iriarte's *Reflexiones* until its inclusion in the *Obras en verso y prosa*, VIII (Madrid: Imprenta Real, 1805), 7 - 67.

50. MASSON DE MORVILLIERS, [NICOLÁS]. "Espagne," in *Encyclopédie Méthodique, Géographie*, I (Paris: Panckoucke, 1783), 554 - 68. The article that started almost everything that happened in Forner's career from 1783 on.

51. MELÉNDEZ VALDÉS, JUAN. *Batilo: égloga en alabanza de la vida del campo, premiada por la Real Academia Española en junta que celebró el día 18 de marzo de 1780* (Madrid: Joaquín Ibarra, 1780). The poem criticized by Iriarte, item 49, and defended by Forner, item 16.

52. [SAMANIEGO, FÉLIX MARÍA DE]. *Continuación de las memorias críticas de Cosme Damián* (n.p.: n.d. [1785?]). Reprinted in *Obras inéditas o poco conocidas del insigne fabulista D. Félix María de Samaniego*, ed. Estaquio Fernández de Navarrete (Vitoria: Hijos de Manteli, 1866), pp. 135 - 51. The work that elicited from Huerta his *tuerto* comment about Forner in item 44.

53. [SÁNCHEZ, TOMÁS ANTONIO]. *Defensa de D. Fernando Pérez, autor de la "Carta de Paracuellos," impugnado por el licenciado Paulo Ipnocausto. Escríbiala un amigo de D. Fernando* (Madrid: Viuda de Ibarra, 1790). Response to Forner, item 6.

54. ———. *Carta de Paracuellos, escrita por D. Fernando Pérez a un sobrino que se hallaba en peligro de ser autor de un libro* (Madrid: Viuda de Ibarra, 1789). Forner's response to this was item 6.

55. SEMPERE Y GUARINOS, JUAN. *Ensayo de una biblioteca española de los mejores escritores del reynado de Carlos III.* 6 vols. (Madrid: Imprenta Real, 1785 - 89). Forner's *Suplemento* (item 35) was a reply to the Trigueros article in volume VI. The Dolphin Book Company made a facsimile reprint of this work in 1963.

56. [TRIGUEROS, CÁNDIDO MARÍA]. *Las majas: poema chusqui-heroico por D. Melchor María Sánchez Toledano* (Madrid: D. Antonio Espinosa, 1789). Makes sarcastic comments about Forner's *Discursos*, item 19.

57. ————. *La riada: descríbese la terrible inundación que molestó a Sevilla en los últimos días del año 1783 y los primeros de 1784.* (Sevilla: Vázquez y Compañía, 1784. The work to which Forner responded in item 7.

58. VARGAS Y PONCE, JOSÉ. *Declamación contra los abusos introducidos en el castellano, presentada y no premiada en la Academia Española, año de 1791. Síguela una disertación sobre la lengua castellana y la antecede un diálogo que explica el designio de la obra* (Madrid: Viuda de Ibarra, 1793). Forner accused Vargas of plagiarizing Mayans in this work, item 15.

SECONDARY SOURCES

ÁLVAREZ GÓMEZ, JESÚS. *Juan Pablo Forner (1756 - 97): Preceptista y filósofo de la historia* (Madrid: Editora Nacional, 1971). A long commentary on Forner's concept of history, philosophy, and theology. Tends to defend and praise Forner's point of view. The bibliography is filled with inaccuracies in citing items.

ANDIOC, RENÉ. *Sur la querelle du théatre au temps de Leandro Fernández de Moratín* (Tarbes: Saint-Joseph, 1970). A well-documented study of the polemics concerning the theater. Extensive bibliography.

ARAUJO COSTA, L. "Las influencias de Huet sobre Forner," *Revista de literatura*, 4, no. 8 (octubre-diciembre 1953), 307 - 18. An attempt to explain and defend Forner's orthodox theological perspective.

BERTRAND, J. J. A. "Masson de Morvilliers," *Bulletin Hispanique*, 24 (1922), 120 - 24. A brief discussion about the author of the *Encyclopédie* article.

COOK, JOHN A. *Neo-Classic Drama in Spain: Theory and Practice* (Dallas: Southern Methodist University Press, 1959). An interesting presentation of the eighteenth-century theater, with information about Forner's *Filósofo enamorado* and the journal *La Espigadera* (pp. 384 - 92 and pp. 325 - 28).

COTARELO Y MORI, EMILIO. *Bibliografía de las controversias sobre la licitud del teatro en España* (Madrid: Est. Tip. de la "Revista de Archivos, Bibliotecas y Museos," 1904). Covers the theater controversies from 1468 to 1868, and includes the text of several rare pamphlets by Forner (pp. 269 - 319).

————. *Iriarte y su época* (Madrid: Est. Tip. "Sucesores de Rivadeneyra," 1897). The most informative study of eighteenth-century Spanish literature available in any language. The focus is on Iriarte, but there is extensive material about his contemporaries, including Forner.

Cox, R. Merritt. *Tomás de Iriarte* (New York: Twayne Publishers, 1972). Interesting general study of Iriarte, with a review of the critical attitudes toward Iriarte from the eighteenth century to the present.

Cueto, Leopoldo Augusto de. "Bosquejo histórico-crítico de la poesía castellana en el siglo XVIII," *BAE* 61 (Madrid, 1869), pp. v - ccxxxvii. Very detailed history of eighteenth-century poetry. Includes many letters and documents published for the first time.

Estala, Pedro. "Veintiuna cartas inéditas de D. Pedro Estala dirigidas a D. Juan Pablo Forner bajo el nombre arcádico Damón para la historia literaria del último tercio del siglo XVIII," ed. Juan Pérez de Guzmán, *Boletín de la Real Academia de la Historia*, 53 (1911), 5 - 36. Interesting letters to Forner concerning *El filósofo enamorado*, with comments about Forner's other plays.

Fernández González, Francisco. *Historia de la crítica literaria en España desde Luzán hasta nuestros días* (Madrid: Imprenta de D. Alejandro Gómez Fuentenebro, 1867). Valuable study of eighteenth-century and Romantic criticism.

Glendinning, Nigel. *A Literary History of Spain: The Eighteenth Century* (New York: Barnes and Noble, Inc., 1972). An interesting, brief treatment of the period.

González Blanco, A. "Ensayo sobre un crítico español del siglo XVIII," *Nuestro tiempo*, 17 (1917), 157 - 70. One of the first articles devoted entirely to Forner.

Herr, Richard. *The Eighteenth Century Revolution in Spain* (Princeton: Princeton University Press, 1958). The best history of the eighteenth century available in English. There is also a Spanish edition published by Aguilar in 1964.

Herrero, Javier. *Los orígenes del pensamiento reaccionario español* (Madrid: Editorial Cuadernos para el Diálogo, 1973). A fascinating study which takes the point of view that the traditionalist ideas of eighteenth-century Spain are not Spanish, but part of the worst European conservative currents. Herrero attacks his fellow Hispanists with a vigor worthy of Forner himself.

Jiménez Salas, María. *Vida y obras de D. Juan Pablo Forner y Segarra* (Madrid: Consejo Superior de Investigaciones Científicas, 1944). Invaluable for its extensive documentation and reproduction of texts, but the adulatory point of view is lacking in objectivity.

Jurado, José. "Repercusiones del pleito con Iriarte en la obra literaria de Forner," *Thesaurus: Boletín del Instituto Caro y Cuervo*, 24 (1969), 228 - 77. A detailed presentation of Forner's disputes with Iriarte.

LAUGHRIN, MARÍA FIDELIA. *Juan Pablo Forner As a Critic* (Washington, D. C.: Catholic University Press, 1943). The first book devoted entirely to Forner. A sketchy, very positive treatment.

MARAVALL, J. A. "El sentimiento de nación en el siglo 18: la obra de Forner," *La torre*, año 15, no. 57 (julio-septiembre 1967), pp. 25 - 56. One of the best interpretations of Forner's political ideology, presented with objectivity.

McCLELLAND, IVY L. *Ignacio de Luzán* (New York: Twayne Publishers, 1973). A good, concise study of the author of the *Poética* (1737), the principle treatise on neoclassic poetry in eighteenth-century Spain.

MARÍAS, JULIÁN. *La España posible en tiempo de Carlos III* (Madrid: Sociedad de Estudios y Publicaciones, 1963). An excellent, perceptive study of liberal trends in Forner's time, with a discussion of Forner as the reactionary.

MENÉNDEZ Y PELAYO, MARCELINO. *Historia de las ideas estéticas en España,* ed. Enrique Sánchez Reyes. 5 vols. (Vols. 1 - 5 of the Edición Nacional de las Obras Completas de Menéndez Pelayo) (Santander: Aldus, S. A. de Artes Gráficas, 1957). See pp. 302 - 36 of volume 3 for a discussion of Forner and his polemics by this well-known traditionalist historian of Spanish literature.

————. *Historia de los heterodoxos españoles,* ed. Enrique Sánchez Reyes. 8 vols. (Vols. 35 - 42 of the Edición Nacional de las Obras Completas de Menéndez Pelayo) (Santander: Aldus, S. A. de Artes Gráficas, 1957). See pp. 386 - 95 for a discussion of Andrés Piquer and Forner.

MONGUIÓ, LUIS. "Fray Diego Tadeo González and Spanish Taste in Poetry in the 18th Century," *Romanic Review,* 52 (1961), 241 - 60. The interest in sixteenth-century poetry shown by Fray Diego, whose Salamanca *tertulia* included Forner.

PELLISIER, ROBERT E. *The Neo-Classic Movement in Spain During the XVIII Century.* Leland Stanford Junior University Publications University Series, No. 30 (Palo Alto: Stanford University Press, 1918). Interesting, brief presentation of the period.

PEÑUELAS, MARCELINO C. "Personalidad y obra de Forner," *Hispanófila,* 26 (1966), 23 - 31. A well-written, general discussion of Forner's literary personality, but presents no new insights or observations.

PINTA LLORENTE, MIGUEL DE LA. "El sentido de la cultura española en el siglo XVIII e intelectuales de la época (aportaciones inéditas)," *Revista de estudios políticos,* no. 68 (marzo-abril 1953), pp. 79 - 114. Interesting discussion of intellectual currents, with emphasis on Forner's contemporaries.

PIQUER Y ARRUFAT, ANDRÉS. "Informe de la Academia Médica-matritense al supremo Consejo de Castilla sobre censores de libros," in *Obras póstumas,* ed. Juan Crisóstomo Piquer (Madrid: Ibarra, 1785), pp. 210 - 20. The ideas on government censorship held by Forner's uncle, who was responsible for his early education.

Rossi, Guiseppe Carlo. *Estudios sobre las letras en el siglo XVIII*, trans. Jesús López Pacheco (Madrid: Gredos, 1967). Includes the Spanish version of the following item.

———. "La teórica del teatro in Juan Pablo Forner," *Filologia romanza*, 5 (1958), 210 - 22. A discussion of Forner's dramatic theory, based on the *Exequias de la lengua castellana*.

Rubio, Antonio. *La crítica del galicismo en España (1726 - 1832)* (México: Universidad Nacional de México, 1937). Discussion of attitudes toward the French. Article on Forner, pp. 89 - 97.

———. "Comments on 18th Century *Purismo*," *Hispanic Review*, 3 (1935), 317 - 30. A briefer presentation in English of the previous item.

Sarrailh, Jean. *L'Espagne éclairée de la seconde moitié du XVIIIe siécle* (Paris: Imprimer Nationale, 1954). A comprehensive study of society and literature in the second half of the eighteenth century in Spain. Extensive bibliography of primary and secondary sources.

———. *La España ilustrada de la segunda mitad del siglo XVIII* (México and Buenos Aires: Fondo de Cultura Económica, 1957). Spanish edition of the above.

Simón Díaz, José. "Documentos referentes a escritores españoles del siglo XVIII," *Revista de bibliografía nacional*, 5 (1944), 472 - 78. Interesting documents concerning the censor's comments on *El asno erudito* and *Para casos tales*.

———. "Los últimos trabajos de Forner," *Revista de bibliografía nacional*, 7 (1946), 376 - 78. A brief notation about the things found in Forner's home after his death.

Sotelo, Joaquín María. "Elogio del señor don Juan Pablo Forner," in *BAE*, 63 (Madrid, 1871), 272 - 97. The first commentary on Forner, delivered several weeks after his death. The information in this eulogy has been the source for most of the biographical studies on Forner.

Spell, Jefferson Rhea. *Rousseau in the Spanish World Before 1833* (Austin: University of Texas Press, 1938). Includes a good bibliography of works dealing with French influence in Spain.

Villanueva, Luis. "Biografía española: Juan Pablo Forner," *Seminario pintoresco español*, 9 (1844), 129 - 31; 142 - 43.

———. "Vida y escritos del autor," in *Obras de Juan Pablo Forner*, pp. ix - xxii. This biographical sketch is a variation on the previous item, and is reprinted as a "Noticia bibliográfica" in *BAE*, 63 (Madrid, 1871), 263 - 67.

Zamora Vicente, A. "La *Oración apologética* de Juan Pablo Forner," in *De Garcilaso a Valle-Inclán* (Buenos Aires: Editorial Sudamericana, 1950), pp. 149 - 81. A reprint of the prologue to Zamora's edition of the *Oración apologética*.

Zavala, Iris M. "Forner y Blanco: dos vertientes del XVIII," *Cuadernos americanos*, 148, no. 5 (septiembre-octubre 1966), pp. 128 - 38. Deals with the relationship between Forner and Blanco White, and their differing points of view.

————. "Francia en la poesía del XVIII español," *Bulletin Hispanique*, 68 (1966), 49 - 68. The political, anti-French poetry of various writers, including Forner.

Index